ROGER PLANT was born in England in 1947. Since 1971
he has travelled extensively in Latin America. He resided in
Colombia for several months in 1971 while re-searching for
a thesis on problems of rural education and in 1972 he
gained a B.Phil. in Latin American studies at Oxford
University. Between 1972-75 he worked in the Latin
American Department of Amnesty International, and in
November 1973 was a member of the Amnesty delegation
to Chile. From 1975-76 he worked in the administration of
development programmes in Central America and the
Caribbean, and was in Guatemala City at the time of the
February 1976 earthquake. He is now working on a study
of the relationship between human rights and development
in rural Latin America under the sponsorship of the
Committee of Indigenous Peoples of the Anti-Slavery
Society.

Dedication

In memory of Mario Lopez Larrave and the 'disappeared' people of Guatemala.

GUATEMALA
UNNATURAL DISASTER

ROGER PLANT

Latin America Bureau
Research and action on Latin America

First published in Great Britain in 1978 by

The Latin America Bureau
P O Box 134
London NW1 4J Y

ISBN 0 906156 01 7

Printed by The Trade Printing Company Ltd.,
24-25 Cowcross St., London EC1

Contents

Preface

The Central American republic of Guatemala occasionally hits the
headlines of the British press — when there is a natural disaster, a
particularly violent kidnapping, a presidential changeover or when
Guatemalan troops are threatening to invade the neighbouring British
colony of Belize. Such dramatic events give little or no insight into
the reality of Guatemalan society today — the gross inequalities, the
desperate poverty and the political violence and repression.

The Latin America Bureau commissioned this report in an attempt to
provide such an insight. In particular, many of those involved in relief
programmes following the February 1976 earthquake in Guatemala
were anxious that the appalling effects of the disaster should be seen
in their true perspective — as much a consequence of the underlying
structural injustices of Guatemalan society as of the physical impact
of the earthquake itself.

At the same time, the issue of human rights has gained international
prominence and has become an important consideration in foreign
policy decisions in the West. However, human rights violations cannot
be regarded simply in terms of overt political repression but must also
be seen in the context of the country's social, economic and political
systems which give rise to such repression.

We hope that this report will contribute to an understanding of
Guatemalan society and to the current debate on human rights
considerations in foreign aid decisions.

Latin America Bureau
January 1978

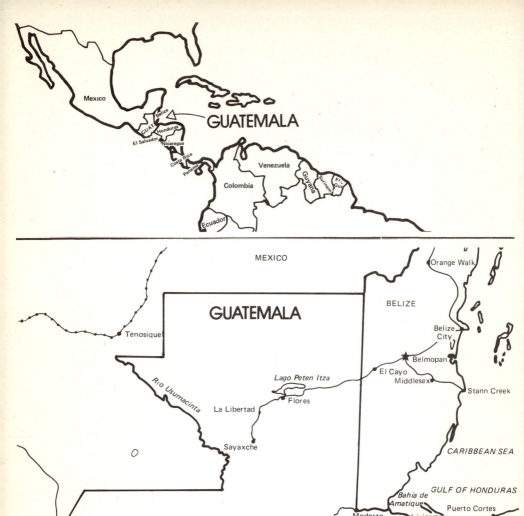

MEXICO

GUATEMALA

BELIZE

Orange Walk

Belize City

Belmopan

El Cayo
Middlesex

Stann Creek

Tenosique

Lago Peten Itza

Flores

La Libertad

Rio Usumacinta

Sayaxche

CARIBBEAN SEA

GULF OF HONDURAS

Bahia de Amatique

Puerto Cortes

Modesto Mendez

Livingston

Santo Tomas de Castilla

Francisco Vela

Lago de Izabal

El Estor

Ciudad Cuauhtemoc

Coban

HONDURAS

Inter-American

Huehuetenango

Santa Cruz del Quiche

Salama

Rio Hondo

Zacapa

San Marcos

Totonicapan

El Progreso

Chiquimula

Highway

Quezaltenango

Solola

Chimaltenango

Jalapa

Coatepeque

Lago de Atitlan

Mazatenango

GUATEMALA

Ciudad Tecun Uman

Antigua Guatemala

Asuncion Mita

Ocos

Retalhuleu

Escuintla

Champerico

Cuilapa

Tiquisate

San Jose

Iztapa

Santa Ana

Tecojate

San Salvador

PACIFIC OCEAN

EL SALVADOR

GUATEMALA

———	International Boundary
★	National capital
•–•–•	Railway
———	Road

0 10 20   40 Miles

0 10 20   40 Kilometers

A Statistical Outline

Area		Approx. 42,000 sq. miles or 108,900 sq. km. (England = 50,300 sq. miles)
Population	Total	5,395,000 (1975)
	Growth	2.8% (1960-1974)
	Rural	66.4% of total population (1974)
The People	Race	43.3% (1964) Indians of Mayan extraction concentrated in the West-Central Highlands.
		Remainder: *ladino* (those of mixed Spanish and Indian descent — *mestizos* — and culturally assimilated Indians)
	Languages	Official language: Spanish 17 major Indian languages including Quiche, Cakchiquel, Mam. Kekchi.
	Religion	Over 95% Roman Catholic, but with considerable native syncretism.
Main Cities	Capital	Ciudad de Guatemala (pop. 800,000)
	Others	Escuintla, Quezaltenango
Economy		GNP (1975) Total: US $3,530 million Per capita: US $650

Income & Land Distribution	5% of pop. receives average annual income of US $2,189 per capita.
	50% of pop. receives an average of US $81 per capita (1970).
	2.1% of landowners own 72.2% of land.
	91.4% of landowners own 21.9% of land (1964)
Labour	20% of labour force is unemployed; under-employment estimated at 52%.
	1.6% of labour force is unionised (1974)
Recent Governments	Jorge Ubico (1931-1944)
	Juan Jose Arevalo (1945-1951)
	Jacobo Arbenz (1951-1954)
	Castillo Armas (1954-1957)
	Miguel Ydigoras Fuentes (1958-1963)
	Enrique Peralta Azurdia (1963-1966)
	Julio Cesar Mendez Montenegro (1966-1970)
	Carlos Arana Osorio (1970-1974)
	Kjell Laugerud (1974-

Introduction

Guatemala is a small Central American country about which little is known in Britain. The two countries do not even have diplomatic relations, owing to a long-standing diplomatic conflict over Belize, the neighbouring country to which Guatemala has many times claimed territorial rights. Press coverage of Guatemala in Britain has normally been limited to articles on this conflict, to Guatemala's threats of invasion and the British response. But on 4 February 1976 Guatemala was struck by a severe earthquake — perhaps the worst natural disaster in its history — that claimed over 22,000 lives and rendered over one million homeless out of a total population of five and a half million. Journalists and television teams flooded in from all over the world, including Britain, and for a few brief weeks Guatemala received a hitherto unparalleled amount of coverage in the world press. At the same time the Disaster Emergency Committee in Britain launched a special appeal for Guatemala, which brought in over £1¼ million for allocation by five major British charities. Official British aid was rejected, because of the Belize dispute, but the private donations were welcomed. Generous donations and credits were given by other governments, inter-governmental and private organisations. The US Congress, for example, voted an emergency US $25,000,000 for relief and reconstruction work through the US Agency for International Development (AID). The Inter-American Development Bank and Central American Bank for Economic Integration allocated $38,900,000, and the World Bank $20,000,000 within weeks of the earthquake.

Within Guatemala, although the international aid at a time of tragedy was welcomed by everyone, concern was expressed by many that the earthquake should be seen in its true perspective. The dimensions of the disaster were as great as they were precisely because of the structural injustice of Guatemalan society. Though the physical force of the earthquake struck urban and rural areas and the poor shanty towns of Guatemala City, the wealthy residential and commercial sectors emerged almost unscathed because expensive homes and offices had been built to withstand earthquake tremors. Moreover it was frequently pointed out that the suffering caused by the earthquake, great though it was, was little more severe than the unnatural disaster that had afflicted the Guatemalan population over the previous decade. While the earthquake killed 22,000, over 15,000 died between 1970-74 at the hands of right-wing terrorist groups officially condoned by the government of Carlos Arana. Many more again have died from malnutrition resulting from the grossly inegalitarian land-tenure system and the unequal distribution of wealth and opportunity. Within weeks of the earthquake, tortured bodies were found by the roadside and two members of Guatemala's opposition parties were machine-gunned in Guatemala City in the midst of reconstruction work. In the labour sector, union organisers were dismissed from their jobs and at the same time Guatemala's President attacked the trade union movement as the "enemy of reconstruction".

Although the idea of this report evolved from the February 1976 earthquake, it is not so much an account of the earthquake itself as of the Guatemala that was hit by it. Beginning from the disaster which aroused so much international concern, the report proceeds to an analysis of the less widely publicised political violence. Next it considers the two sectors which have suffered most of all from this violence, namely the urban trade union movement and the peasantry. The third chapter demonstrates how politically powerful groups have used both legal and extra-legal means to prevent the growth of an independent trade union movement which could challenge their control. The fourth chapter, on the Guatemalan peasantry, takes a more historical approach. It shows how the indigenous population, which had limited but clearly defined rights to the use of common land during the colonial period, has suffered from the institutionalisation of private property over the past 150 years. Land became progressively concentrated in a few hands as extensive land grants were made to individuals willing to concentrate on the cultivation of cash crops for export: first coffee, in the second half of the nineteenth century, then sugar, bananas, cotton in more recent years, while cattle ranching, primarily for meat exports to the US market, is once again on the increase. In Guatemala commercial cash crop farming has never been heavily mechanised, for landowners have preferred to rely on the readily available supply of low-cost permanent and seasonal labour. Though repressive legislation was needed until the 1930s to force peasant farmers to undertake seasonal labour, the land tenure situation has for long been so acute that farmers in many provinces have been reduced to a sub-subsistence level, and have had no option but to undertake grossly underpaid seasonal labour in order to survive.

The fourth chapter also analyses the one period in Guatemalan history (1944-54) when a serious attempt was made to find a peaceful solution to these problems. The two governments of Juan Jose Arevalo and Jacobo Arbenz had sought first to enforce minimum work standards in urban and rural areas, second to enact a serious land reform involving the distribution of all national land and unused or underutilised private land, and third to encourage the growth of labour unions and peasant organisations. The reforms proved unacceptable both to the landowning classes and to the US government, whose economic interests in Guatemala were threatened. In 1954 Jacobo Arbenz was overthrown by a US-backed military coup which reversed the agrarian reform, outlawed the labour unions, and paved the way for what has with one brief exception until the present day been direct military rule.

Contemporary political violence in Guatemala can only be understood in this context. As the reports of international organisations (including the International Labour Organisation and the Organisation of American States) have repeatedly argued, there can be no long-term political alternative to agrarian reform and a significant increase in wages in the rural sector. Although the urban sector has grown over the past twenty years, Guatemala City is still the only major town.

In Guatemala City, as in other Latin American capitals, there is a high incidence of unemployment and underemployment, and for the foreseeable future well over 50% of the population will have to live off the land. Successive governments since 1954 have not only ignored demands for land reform, but have allowed even greater concentration of land in a few hands, and have made no effort to prevent the eviction of peasants from land under dispute. Rather, they have facilitated discrimination against the peasantry and indigenous population by systematically preventing the resurgence of the peasant organisations which had played such an important part in the land reform process of the early 1950s. In the late 1960s and early 1970s in particular, after a left-wing guerrilla movement had penetrated rural areas, the military and officially tolerated right-wing terrorist groups reacted by killing the thousands of peasant leaders who had in any way been involved in organisational work.

Since 1973, events in Chile and Argentina have outraged public opinion throughout the world. Guatemala, a poorer and strategically less important country, has been largely forgotten. But in many ways there are disturbing parallels between the overthrow of democracy in Chile and Guatemala. In September 1973 the democratically elected Marxist President Allende of Chile was violently overthrown with United States intervention following three years of government which had enacted substantial land reforms, permitted the increase of trade union activities under Communist leadership, and expropriated US assets in the interests of national economic development. After Allende's overthrow the military junta of Chile reversed the land reform, outlawed the Chilean TUC and claimed (impossibly) that its aim was to restore the conditions that had prevailed before 1970. After three years of widespread torture and political imprisonment, the junta decided to rid itself of the embarassment of political prisoners. Over the past year, political opponents of the regime have tended simply to 'disappear' after abduction by the junta's security services. To the Guatemalans all of this must sound disturbingly familiar. Such political 'disappearances', now common in Chile and Argentina, originated in Guatemala.

Over the past year much attention has been paid to the human rights initiatives of US President Carter. If there is one country where the impact of this foreign policy should and could be felt, it is Guatemala. It was the first independent country in Latin America to suffer the effects of US military intervention; it is, together with the other small Central American republics, the country most completely dependent on the United States at all levels; and geographically it is very close to the United States, being separated from it only by Mexico. But paradoxically it could also be argued that a US President and US Congress, determined to apply human rights criteria in their foreign aid policies, are least able to influence events in countries where US influence and investment has traditionally been strongest. The US administration is now pledged to restricting military and economic aid to repressive governments, but it has so far made no moves to curtail private US investment in such countries. Though official US military and economic aid to Guatemala has been important in the past, it is now an insignificant percentage of total private and multinational investment in that country. The final chapter of this report analyses international human rights initiatives, and particularly US ones, in Latin America as a whole and Guatemala in particular. It discusses the limitations of these initiatives, and looks at some of the issues which have to be faced if international pressure is to have an effect on one of the most repressive countries in contemporary Latin America.

1. The Effects of an Earthquake

1. The Facts about the Earthquake

On 4 February 1976, in the early hours of the morning, the Central American Republic of Guatemala was struck by a savage earthquake, measuring 7.5 degrees on the Richter scale, which caused appalling loss of life and material damage. Of a total population of approximately 5,500,000, over 22,000 were killed, more than 77,000 injured and over 1,000,000 made homeless. It was the severest natural catastrophe in Central America during the twentieth century.

Almost the entire country was affected. Whereas the 1972 earthquake in Nicaragua had struck only the capital city, this catastrophe affected no less than sixteen of Guatemala's twenty-two provinces. In the province of Chimaltenango in the central highlands, inhabited mainly by Indian small farmers and rural workers, 41,677 out of 42,794 homes were destroyed. In the provinces of El Progreso and Zacapa in the eastern lowlands 10,737 homes out of 15,743 and 14,288 out of 20,989 respectively were destroyed. The poorer districts of Guatemala City were equally badly affected.

2. The Social Dimension

Despite the severity of the disaster, the residential, commercial and large industrial sectors of Guatemala City and the country as a whole were barely touched. The agro-industrial structure equally escaped the consequences. The vast sugar, cotton and coffee estates, producing the export crops which bring in Guatemala's foreign exchange, are concentrated in the coastal and south-eastern areas, the two areas least affected by the earthquake. The only significant damage for this sector was the destruction of wharf facilities at Puerto Barrios (from which bananas are exported to the USA), and the collapse of a large bridge on the main highway from Guatemala City to this same port.

In Guatemala City the social nature of the disaster was at its most striking. The numerous residential districts were virtually unaffected. The city is on a well-known fault line that has experienced innumerable earthquakes, major and minor, over the past hundred years. All those who could afford it had constructed earthquake-resistant housing or industrial premises, and were thus largely unaffected. By contrast, many of the poorer districts were devastated. In the marginal squatter settlements of 'La Trinidad' and 'El Gallito' perched perilously on the edge of ravines, adobe huts plummeted down the slopes as the volcanic soil gave way. Many of the inhabitants were self-employed artisan workers, who lost their livelihood along with their homes. An estimated 45,000 artisans were affected.

Within days of the earthquake, the chambers of commerce and industry were able to announce that the productive sector had not suffered serious damage. Though 147 industrial establishments reported some adverse effects, they were rarely major. Productivity was halted above all by the national loss of electricity in the two days after the 'quake, and by the widespread fear caused by the continuing tremors in the days after 4th February. For management the problems were primarily social, since the labour force came predominantly from the affected areas. The prime concern of management could be seen in a large publicity campaign designed to normalise production as soon as possible. "Reconstruction without loss of production" was the prevailing slogan of the day . . .

From today onwards we need more action and less tears. We need to get into shirt sleeves and to sweat, to sweat, work and reconstruct. From today onwards the national slogan is reconstruction without loss of production . . . God is on our side, God is Guatemalan . . .

But such propaganda ignored one major question. Production and reconstruction for whom, and at what cost? The earthquake occurred at a time of growing labour unrest, when workers were taking advantage of the degree of support for trade union freedom professed by President Kjell Laugerud (under his predecessor, President Carlos Arana, virtually no independent trade union activity had been permitted). Groups had been organising within many industrial establishments, in attempts to gain legal recognition for labour unions. Unions members were protected by law against unfair dismissal only after the union's legal status (*personeria juridica*) had been officially recognised by the Ministry of Labour; and in many cases management had dismissed organised workers before this legal status was granted. The pattern was repeated in the immediate aftermath of the earthquake. In one textile factory 120 workers (all the unofficial union members) were dismissed in the week of the earthquake. In one food factory, management was reportedly assisted by the National Police in carrying out arbitrary dismissals. The pattern was to be repeated many times over the coming months. There can be no doubt that the earthquake had strong repercussions on the development of the labour movement in Guatemala. Labour unrest was by no means caused by the disaster, but was significantly accentuated by it. When arbitrary dismissal occurred on top of personal tragedy, the events took on greater political dimensions, and attracted a greater degree of popular and media support for the dismissed workers than had previously been the case (see Chapter III).

3. A Violent Response

The shanty towns of Guatemala City, destroyed by the earthquake, had been as miserable as any in Latin America. Many of them were on private lots whose owners had permitted temporary squatter settlement in makeshift huts but not the construction of stable housing. Moreover the owners, to keep their land assets as liquid as possible, had not permitted the establishment of services of any kind. There was no lighting, no drainage, no running water, no sanitation, in many areas no roads. Ironically, the location of the squatter settlements was the result of an earlier earthquake of 1917; the residential districts had taken up all available land on the city outskirts, leaving only the dangerous ravine areas for squatter settlement.

For the vast numbers of squatters in particular, the earthquake of February 1976 posed an insoluble problem. The ravine areas were a mass of rubble and fallen earth, and further settlement there was prohibited on safety grounds. There was nowhere for these people to go. While some families set up improvised tents and huts in the few public parks or by the roadside, others moved to vacant privately-owned lots. In normal times land invasions would be met with violence, and after the earthquake the response was little different. On 20 February 1976 Rolando Andrade Pena, a leading municipal official and prominent member of the FUR opposition party[1], was machine-gunned to death in the middle of Guatemala City. Though the assassination may have had wider political motives, it was widely believed that his murder was due to the support he had given to the invasion of private land. At about the same time, leaders of the squatter invasions were arrested without warrant (some people believe that their lives were saved only by the protest rally convened straight after their arrest). On February 23rd came more signs that the invasion of private land would not be tolerated by the authorities. Twenty-five families who had settled on the San Julian estate in one of the affected zones were forced off by the national police, this time without violence or reprisals.

On the same day, a journalist from the daily newspaper *El Grafico* observed that the death of Rolando Andrade Pena, and an attack on Christian Democrat party headquarters during the same week, signified a return to 'political normality'. In the month after the earthquake there were over fifty such assassinations (many of them accompanied by torture), giving rise to press reports that a 'Death Squad' of off-duty policemen had resumed its activities. As with the arbitrary labour dismissals, the violence and intimidation after the earthquake was only a repetition of traditional patterns, and the victims were predominantly from the same sectors. The right-wing political terror, like the earthquake, barely affected the wealthy of Guatemala City, the businessmen or the landowners.

4. The Earthquake and the Peasantry

Statistically, the sector most calamitously affected by the earthquake was the highland peasantry. Remote villages were devastated, particularly in the central highland provinces of Chimaltenango and Sacatepequez, and the lowland areas of Zacapa and El Progreso. In the short term, relief problems were accentuated by the virtual inaccessibility of many villages cut off by landslides. But within a

---

1. *Frente Unido de la Revolucion*, a centre-left opposition party which, though strong in the capital city, has so far been unable to obtain formal registration.

few days a massive inflow of emergency aid (particularly from church and voluntary organisations) helped to relieve food, medical and shelter problems in many highland areas. It was in the devastated villages around Chimaltenango that much of the non-governmental foreign aid went in the provision of food and urgently needed construction and roofing materials, which were distributed at subsidised cost in this area through the existing cooperative organisations. In many ways the relief organisations performed an outstanding task in alleviating human suffering in the months after the earthquake. But two factors stand out as a measure of the marginality of the Guatemalan peasant to the national economy and society. First that, when whole provinces inhabited by small farmers had been devastated, it could still be claimed that national agricultural production had not been seriously affected. Second that, in a country where peasant organisation had been one of the strongest in Latin America some twenty years earlier, the relief work had to be entrusted largely to foreign organisations. Whole areas were allocated to foreign governments and private organisations, who were given freedom to conduct relief and reconstruction work according to their own philosophies. The degree of popular participation often depended exclusively on the good will and political sense of the individual relief organisations.

Statistics of loss of life and property indicate the scale of the physical destruction. Other factors must also be taken into account. Marketing and storage facilities were also destroyed, affecting the small agricultural surplus that the subsistence farmer needed at harvest time. One estimate within fifteen days of the earthquake gave a deficit of 500,000 *quintales* of maize and 200,000 *quintales* of beans (the two staple foods of the peasant farmer)[2]. Moreover, the earthquake came at a time when many of the small farmers were customarily away from home performing the annual period of seasonal migratory labour on the coastal estates. Those who left the estates were given no compensation, and the loss of surplus income could be as crucial as the loss of the home itself.

In some cases, the estate owners themselves were concerned to protect their labour supply. And it was significant that the Herrera and Castillo families, the two Guatemalan families to make a substantial contribution to rural reconstruction, concentrated on the rebuilding of their *fincas de mozos* in the highlands (farms kept as a labour reserve by the large landowners, who allow landless labourers to cultivate plots there on the condition that they work on their estates during harvest time).

Within weeks of the earthquake, the rural sector was once again the victim of widespread violence. In the badly affected province of Quiche, the Guatemalan army was carrying out counter-insurgency operations at the same time as relief organisations were involved in reconstruction. On 19 and 20 March 1976, in response to reports of subversive activities, a group of armed men in civilian clothes passed through military roadblocks and kidnapped nine men from the

2. *Quintal* — common Latin American unit of weight approximately equal to 100lbs.

villages of Cotzal, Chajul and Nebaj. They have since disappeared. Despite the protests of opposition members and church officials, there was no official investigation into the disappearances. Again, this was but a return to 'political normality'. In July 1975 over thirty peasants had 'disappeared' from the small village of Xalbal de Ixcan Grande, Quiche province, in the course of a military offensive against alleged guerrilla activity. And in January 1976, just one month before the earthquake, church leaders denounced the arbitrary assassination of four peasants in Chisec, Alta Verapaz, by members of the Border Patrol (*Guardia de Hacienda*).

Many observers were impressed by the stoical courage with which the Guatemalan peasantry set about repairing the earthquake damage. But they have long been inured to such hardship and persecution. We have compared the loss of lives through the earthquake with those through physical violence; but many more lives again are lost through poor and often non-existent medical treatment, and also the serious food shortages that have affected the peasantry in recent years. Even without drought conditions, cases of child mortality are rarely much under 20,000 per year; while according to surveys of the Nutrition Institute for Central America and Panama (INCAP) three-quarters of Guatemalan children under five suffer from malnutrition[3]. Of the thousands of homes destroyed, the majority were classified in a recent census as grossly inadequate[4]. Educational facilities are rudimentary or non-existent, and the level of rural illiteracy is one of the highest in Latin America[5]. Since the overthrow of the reformist Arbenz government in 1954, and the reversal of the 1952 agrarian reform, the destruction of the peasant movement has ensured that peasants have little access to land, credit or the services of national development institutions. Though advances have been made in recent years through the cooperative movement, a relatively small sector of the peasantry (and only the property-owning peasantry) has benefited from this (see Chapter IV). In one sense everything, and in another sense almost nothing, had been lost.

5. The Politics of Reconstruction

In the words of some critics, the earthquake served to 'remove the mask' from Guatemala's face, and reveal the true nature of social injustice. While this was plainest in Guatemala City, where the rich and poor lived a few yards apart, it was equally true (if not so evident) in the rural areas.

In the first days after February 4th, the government showed its good intentions in confronting the immediate emergency. There were none of the allegations so rife after the earthquake of December 1972 in the nearby country

3. Quoted in NACLA report, *Guatemala,* 1974, p.25.
4. *El Desarrollo Integrado de Centro America en la Presente Decada, Tomo 7, Politica Social,* SIECA/BID-INTAL, Buenos Aires, 1973. In 1970 there was a deficit of 612,500 homes, of which 435,900 (71.2%) were in the rural areas. Housing deficit involved not only the lack of housing but inadequate living conditions in existing homes.
5. In the 1964 census the official illiteracy figures were 63.3% with 78.8% of the rural population classified as illiterate.

of Nicaragua, where relief supplies were reportedly stolen by government and police officials. Food and medical supplies were allocated swiftly to relief organisations who were permitted the necessary independence with which to conduct their work.

But the immediate emergency relief, despite its obvious importance, was politically a simpler task than long-term reconstruction. In the latter there were far greater resources to be allocated, and far greater political interests at stake. President Laugerud affirmed at the outset that his government's long-term policy was not only to restore the physical infrastructure of the country, but to "diminish poverty" and "eliminate the segregation of marginal groups from all wealth, all opportunity and all hope of economic, spiritual and cultural advancement". The aim was to be the "promotion and realisation of genuine progress in the development of the popular sectors, urban as well as rural".

In these words the Guatemalan president was perhaps accepting the arguments of radical critics, that the old Guatemala was barely worth reconstructing. But at the same time President Laugerud was careful to mollify his right-wing critics and stress that in his reconstruction policies, as in his overall development policies, he would not attack the landed and wealthy classes but would seek the creation of new wealth rather than the redistribution of existing wealth. "The essence of my politics does not substitute wealth, neither in law nor in the structure of property. Opportunities for progress, for advance in development, for access to better living standards . . . are being achieved and will continue to be achieved without the destruction of wealth already created". At the same time the President appealed for national unity between management and labour sectors, and for an end to the political violence that had plagued the country for the past decade.

The composition of the Reconstruction Committee was an important factor in that partisan political interests were bound to be represented. After an initial power struggle, in which supporters of ex-President Arana vied for control of emergency operations through a National Emergency Committee, this was replaced by a National Reconstruction Committee including more progressive military figures and a broad spectrum of conservative and moderate politicians. Although several members of the Reconstruction Committee were subject to harassment and death threats from right-wing extremist groups, the Committee held together and was able to dictate the reconstruction policies. In housing, these policies involved the provision of low interest loans through the National Agricultural Development Bank (BANDESA) and the National Housing Bank (BANVI). BANDESA and BANVI sold essential building materials to individual farmers and townspeople at cost price, to offset the rapid rise in price since the earthquake. Within months of the earthquake, BANVI also purchased land in four districts of Guatemala City and in neighbouring towns to provide new settlements for the homeless, and financed the construction of emergency housing settlements in affected areas of Guatemala City. Substantial funds were injected into BANVI, through multi-million dollar loans from the International Bank for Reconstruction and Development — IBRD (World Bank), the Inter-American

Development Bank — IDB, and the emergency aid branch — FONDEM — of the Organisation of American States.

Rural and urban housing was only one part of the reconstruction programme, although an important one. Substantial funds were allocated for the repairs of Guatemala's main arteries, particularly the important highway to the Atlantic coast; to repairs of the wharf facilities at the Atlantic ports themselves; to urban amenities including water and lighting; to government buildings; to commerce and services; to social service facilities (mainly in urban areas); and to industry. Only fractionally more than one per cent was to be allocated to agriculture in the first government estimate.

We have seen that one of President Laugerud's stated objectives was to use the reconstruction programme to eliminate the segregation of marginal groups and promote the development of 'popular sectors'. But there is a crucial difference between a programme which purports to represent the interests of popular sectors, and one in which popular movements can play a major part in decision-making and in the determination of priorities. His government certainly attempted to work through the cooperative movement in rural areas, while BANDESA maintained close links with the cooperatives in the allocation of funds for rural housing. But beyond this there appears to have been little genuine popular participation in reconstruction planning, simply because in most rural areas there was no independent peasant organisation, and in urban areas worker organisations had become increasingly identified with the political opposition.

Within a short time of the earthquake it was made abundantly clear that popular organisations were only encouraged (or even tolerated) if they accepted the overall framework of government policies. The trade union movement, no less than political parties and church organisations, attempted to gain influence through its own reconstruction work. But whereas political parties did so by concentrating on material aid — sometimes to the point of granting money or materials only to their own affiliates — the trade union leadership in carrying out its legitimate functions needed to go further. At first this involved protests and strikes after arbitrary dismissals and resurgent political violence; later it included demands for better working conditions, access to social services, higher salaries and an end to illegal sanctions against union organisers. The government predictably responded by using the emergency conditions after the earthquake to attack the trade unions as the "enemies of reconstruction" (see Chapter III).

In these circumstances, the Guatemalan government's appeals for national unity during the reconstruction period were bound to fall on deaf ears. Government and opposition blamed each other for propagating violence and unrest. While President Laugerud himself appealed for an end to the violence, opposition and trade union sectors formed a National Front against Violence, claiming that its causes could be found within the government's own policies and repressive practices. Within this framework, a large number of international agencies had to decide how best to cope with the substantial social and economic problems caused by the earthquake.

II Violence, Death Squads and Disappearances

1. The Setting for Violence
On 14 July 1976, the Association of University Students of Guatemala, in an
open letter to President Laugerud, called for the formation of a national front
against the organised violence that had plagued the country for a decade.

The Guatemalan people appear to be condemned to ... the daily worry of
hundreds of mothers, wives, sisters etc. who see how their husbands disappear
into the hands of armed bands of men acting with impunity in broad daylight, or
are captured by security forces. With luck the relatives of the kidnapped worker,
peasant or student may find the corpse of their loved one beside some local road.
Those who do not have this 'luck' have to spend entire years waiting for some
news of the missing person. The terror in which we Guatemalans have lived for
ten years is unbearable. At the turn of any corner, at any moment, may appear
that treacherous gunfire that ends courageous lives . . . The people of Guatemala
would like to know the real cause of the violence that appears every day in
Guatemala. For instance, why is there no sign of the engineering student Mario
Poggio, who was captured by security forces at the end of last year, later
released and then recaptured over 50 days ago? Where is the engineering student
Jose Fernando Lobo Dubon? Who abducted Marta Cabrera Ramirez, student of
the Central American Teacher Training College, together with her relatives, last
May 31st? Where are the people responsible for the criminal assault on the Rector
of San Carlos University, Dr Roberto Valdeavellano Pinot? Why has there been
no clarification of acts like the assassination of Rolando Andrade, the assault on
Manuel Colom Argueta, or the harassment of the inhabitants of the 'El Gallito'
district, in which more than 20 youths, women and children were beaten and
insulted by members of the Detective Corps? ... Only three days ago two
university students, Heriberto Luna Velasquez and Jorge Abrahan Castellanos,
were shot dead in the city streets. Groups of men with arms of calibres allocated
only to the military pass through town and countryside totally unmolested. Arms
of the type possessed only by the national army (rockets, grenades, machine-guns
etc.) appear in the hands of civilians ... In the rural sector the Mobile Military
Police (*Policia Militar Ambulante*) has effectively been converted into a private
force of the large farmers and landowners. Moreover, there has still been no
satisfactory answer to the allegations of the existence of a secret organisation
called the Regional Police (*Policia Regional*), whose objective is to spearhead the
repression . . . Workers, peasants, students and teachers, intellectuals, housewives
and all popular sectors, the Association of University Students calls on you to
constitute a National Front against Violence and Repression, as the instrument
to bring to a halt the assassination and violence used against the majority sector
of Guatemala. We university students strongly condemn the organised violence
that has been unleashed on the Guatemalan people since 1954. We condemn the
violence and repression that has cost over 20,000 Guatemalan lives since 1966.

We condemn the complicity of the government security organisations in all acts against the people. We urge a basic respect for human rights in Guatemala.[1]

In the same month of June 1976 Rene de Leon Schlotter, President of Guatemala's Christian Democrat party and one of the country's leading agrarian lawyers, appeared as the major witness on Guatemala at hearings held by the US Congress in Washington on the human rights situation in Central America. De Leon Schlotter likewise asserted that the violence had become endemic; that the protagonists were essentially right-wing groups; and that this violence was used as an intimidatory measure to prevent the rise of a democratic political opposition:

Another feature of this phenomenon is that it comes mainly from the right: for instance, *La Mano,* the National Organised Anti-Communist Movement (*Movimiento Anticomunista Nacional Organizado* — MANO), which identifies its crimes with a white hand. Other groups of the extreme right have used violence as their only tool: the New Anti-Communist Organisation (NOA), Anti-Communist Commando of Guatemala (CADEG), and the death squad which in the name of social morality eliminates common criminals, and — incidentally — their political enemies. The violence organised by these groups has, as I have said, a double purpose: *first* to sow terror and bring the people to their knees in fear of their lives, and to suppress all criticism on the part of the communications media and political or civil groups and of the people in general; in particular, to suppress social activity, such as the unions or simple economic cooperatives. From 1954-75, cooperatives were persecuted in Guatemala as communist or communist-sympathising groups. And *second*, to eliminate opponents; political leaders are killed, labour union leaders are kidnapped, individuals and even their families are persecuted and threatened. In Guatemala, in order to avoid responsibility for unjust and arbitrary sentences, they don't bother with detention; the opponent is killed or 'kidnapped' in the streets and just disappears. The second purpose also helps achieve the first: fear prevails, peasants stay away from the cooperative, citizens stay away from politics, because each of these is a legal but 'dangerous' activity that might potentially work against the dictatorship. A fundamental feature of terror is that it is indiscriminate; anyone can be a victim of the process.[2]

After this broad introduction, de Leon Schlotter went on to describe the separate 'waves' of violence, and attempted to pinpoint those sectors most responsible. He found that the phenomenon began with the arrival in power of the right-wing National Liberation Movement (*Movimiento de Liberacion Nacional* — MLN) in 1954. This was the political party that came to power with

1. From Open Letter of Association of University Students, 14 June 1976. Addressed to: President Laugerud; Interior Minister General Leonel Vassaux Martinez; Defence Minister General Romeo Lucas; Deputies of National Congress; and "workers, peasants, students and the Guatemalan people in general".
2. Dr. Rene de Leon Schlotter, speech before the Subcommittee on International Organisations of the House Committee on International Relations, US Congress, Hearings on Human Rights in Central America, June 1976.

US Government backing, in the coup against President Arbenz. It disappeared almost completely when it lost the elections in 1957, but reappeared on a major scale in 1967, when many MLN leaders enlisted in the counter-insurgency groups operating in the province of Zacapa (where an active guerrilla movement had begun to pose a serious threat to the government). The MLN, said de Leon Schlotter, had taken advantage of their power between 1970-4 to organise small private armies; a process that was facilitated when the Ministry of the Interior approved the Congressional Security Guard credentials for more than 600 people. De Leon Schlotter went on to suggest that Guatemala's President from 1970-4, Colonel Carlos Arana Osorio, was directly responsible for the widespread political violence at this time:

During this period we also saw the participation of the National Police, the Mobile Military Police (*Policia Militar Ambulante*) and the Detective Corps in the crimes, especially kidnappings, in which the victims disappeared forever or appeared, dead, a few days later in faraway places. It would be hard to account for the responsibility of the party in power at this time − the MLN − and of some of the police organisations, without the consent of President Carlos Arana Osorio, who was once Chief of the Military Base in Zacapa, in charge of organising the paramilitary groups that carried out the repression of 1967-8[3].

The hard facts and statistics of Guatemala's political violence have been carefully compiled by Amnesty International (AI), who sent their own delegation there in May 1976, and have also sent a series of submissions concerning Guatemala to the Inter-American Human Rights Commission of the Organisation of American States[4]. Amnesty International cites claims that over 7,000 people disappeared or were found dead in 1971, while over 15,000 were listed as missing in the first three years of the Arana government. Although Amnesty admits that it does not have complete records enabling it to corroborate these figures, the organisation has stated in a recent report that:

Although impossible to verify through individual case dossiers, AI estimates that the total number of deaths and disappearances in Guatemala attributable to official and semi-official forces since 1966, is likely to exceed 20,000. This figure is based on reports from the domestic and international press, government and opposition statements, and AI's own statistical findings. Prior to 1972, AI had recorded the names of over 1,000 Guatemalans reported executed or 'disappeared'. From 1972 up to April 1976, a total of 1,105 individual cases of executions and disappearances were documented. Of this total, 786 were abducted before 'disappearance' or being found dead, while 320 were shot outright.[5]

And although some commentators, including the US Department of State, have claimed that the situation has improved since the days of President Arana,

---

3. Ibid.
4. AI submissions to IACHR, OAS, February 1971-1975.
5. AI International Briefing, *Guatemala*, December 1976, p.11.

other AI statistics would appear to question this. From 1 July 1974 (the date of President Laugerud's inauguration) until April 1976, Amnesty had recorded 379 cases of death and disappearance that appeared to represent extrajudicial executions. Moreover, according to reports collected from the Guatemalan press, over 200 'common criminals' were killed by paramilitary groups in the weeks immediately following the earthquake of February 1976.

Despite allegations from national and international organisations, the governments of Guatemala have in recent years persistently denied responsibility or official complicity. Later in this chapter we shall investigate the trend of political violence since the early 1960s, when a guerrilla movement first emerged in Guatemala (a movement that was wiped out, according to the government itself, by the late 1960s). But it is worth looking briefly at the response of successive governments to allegations of official complicity.

In May 1971, the Inter-American Commission on Human Rights (IACHR) of the Organisation of American States first made representations to the Arana government. The Commission requested an official reply to allegations that since November 1970 over 700 assassinations had been carried out for political reasons by elements that "enjoy complete government protection and therefore act with total impunity". When the Guatemalan government failed to reply, in March 1972 the Commission repeated its request for information. This time the government denied responsibility, and attributed the assassinations to "extremist factions bent on mutual destruction"; it added that the culprits would be brought to justice when captured by the security forces. No information was provided on any of the specific cases mentioned in the allegations.

In September 1972 the Commission sent to the Guatemalan government the names of 300 missing persons, and a summary of the circumstances of their disappearance. The government replied by claiming that some of the persons had not disappeared, and that investigations were still under way to establish the whereabouts of the remainder. In June 1973 the Commission repeated its request for information, and was informed (a) that the Government of Guatemala considered its previous replies to be full and explicit, and (b) that it could not give further details concerning the investigations, as this would alert those responsible and thus facilitate their escape. The government thereby admitted that it *did* have some evidence of the identity of those responsible, even though no-one has ever been brought to trial after such disappearances.

In November 1973 the Commission requested permission to send its own mission of enquiry to Guatemala. This was denied by cable two days later. The then Foreign Minister, Jorge Arenales Catalan, later asserted that the presence of such a mission would constitute a "violation of national sovereignty", and that there were no grounds for such an investigation since the government respected human rights. At its next meeting the IACHR resolved that the allegations should be considered as true, and again urged the government of Guatemala to carry out a full investigation and submit a report to the Commission by September 1974. The chapter was thus unsatisfactorily closed[6]. At approximately the same time,

6. From IACHR archives. Quoted in *INFORPRESS Centroamericano*, 12.6.1974.

when Amnesty International requested information on missing people in Guatemala, officials of the Ministry of the Interior (*Ministerio de Gobernacion*) stated that the actions of this organisation were considered an "intolerable intervention in the internal affairs of the country", motivated "more by political interests than good will to resolve the situation"[7]. Access to investigation is thus denied to national and international bodies. More recently, after the US Congressional hearings of June 1976, the government again made a blanket denial. Though not present at the hearings themselves, the Guatemalan government later addressed a memorandum to US Congress refuting the claims made by Rene de Leon Schlotter and attributing his testimony to partisan political motives. It reads:

With regard to political violence, to which de Leon Schlotter refers, the Government of Guatemala puts on record that this violence is due to the perpetration of criminal acts by groups of extremist ideology obliging the Government of Guatemala to make superhuman efforts for the control and punishment of the terrorists. It was possible for the government in office largely to reduce terrorist activities, because the Government is sufficiently strong, enjoys popular support for controlling the situation through legally constituted National Armed Forces and police authorities. However, it is completely false that the Government tolerates the existence of paramilitary groups ... The persons detained by the police are immediately brought before the judicial authorities, who function in absolute independence of the executive branch of government, and this is followed in each case by trial.

De Leon Schlotter's testimony was written off as "the biased information supplied by de Leon Schlotter, information which is nothing more than his personal assessment or that of the political party, the Christian Democrats, to which he belongs".

After the death or disappearance of any prominent individual, the government condemns the atrocity and announces that full investigations are being carried out, but no more is ever heard. Those who attempt to expose the facts of violence are themselves likely to disappear. A Committee of Relatives of the Disappeared has been established, working in close liaison with the Association of University Students; its legal adviser, Edmundo Guerra Teilheimer, was assassinated in the legal aid centre of San Carlos University in March 1974. In June 1976 when the Rector of this university denounced the increasing post-earthquake violence, an attempt was also made on his life. Congressmen from the Christian Democrat party in particular have at times attempted to summon the Interior Minister to submit to questioning before Congress on these delicate issues. In May 1976, a summons was brought against General Leonel Vassaux Martinez to answer for the "existence and activity of paramilitary groups, peasant massacres in different parts of the country, and recent political crimes in Guatemala". The attempt was frustrated by the united opposition of the right-wing parties. The steering committee (*Junta Directiva*) of Congress ruled that the summons could not go ahead, on the grounds that "the questions formulated did not refer to acts of the government".

7. *INFORPRESS*, 5.6.1974.

Shortly afterwards, in the wake of increasing protests from the recently constituted National Front against Violence, President Laugerud himself felt compelled to make a public statement. In an official communique sent out at the beginning of July 1976, the government pleaded with all Guatemalans to cooperate in the fight againt violence, and . . .

not be taken by surprise by the machinations of extremist groups who, under pretext of fighting violence and criminality, carry out acts which — as the government knows — will be used to create innocent victims for their perverse aims.

The communique then continued, incredibly, to state that the government knew who were guilty of the violence.

Those who think that the government is ignorant of the cause of the increase in violence, and of criminal and political delinquency, are mistaken. And those who think that the government does not know who is responsible are also mistaken. What these people pretend to ignore is that a government which respects law needs convincing proof before it can take proceedings against those responsible, and cannot act arbitrarily under the influence of tendentious accusations or the machinations of extremist politicians[8].

There are two possible reasons for the timing of this surprisingly frank statement. On the one hand, it was made when President Laugerud had become harshly critical of the trade union movement, and was accusing union leaders of disrupting the reconstruction process. On the other hand, it also came at a time when the accusations against one Elias Zimeri (see p.30) provided disturbingly clear evidence of military involvement in political assassinations. Whereas the Laugerud government in 1976 no less than the Arana government in 1973 was claiming that it knew the identity of the culprits, no single act had been taken to dismantle the paramilitary groups that have virtually paralysed open political life in the country.

During the present administration, one person at least claimed that he could name the agents of political assassination. He is now dead, one of the few people to be judicially executed in Guatemala. In April 1975 a national sensation was caused when a former radio-patrol commander of the National Police, Lauro Alvarado y Alvarado (who had been condemned to death for the alleged assassination of a young woman in September 1972) revealed in the death-cell that he had been responsible for the abduction of Humberto Gonzalez Juarez, Armando Braum Valle and Catalina Zambrano on 29 November 1970. All three people had disappeared during the first days of a state of siege declared by President Arana soon after his accession, their bodies being found later in a well near the main Atlantic highway. Lauro Alvarado claimed that he had carried out the abductions on orders from his superiors, and had handed them over to

8. *INFORPRESS*, 15.7.1976.

police intelligence (*Policia Judicial*) who at that time had denied all knowledge of the cases. Lauro Alvarado also informed a journalist that he had carried out the abductions of Santos Landa Castaneda and Carmen Landa Castaneda in 1971 (Carmen was accused of 'subversive activities' but released shortly afterwards; Santos has 'disappeared' since 1971). Shortly after this interview, Lauro Alvarado was declared incommunicado in the prison, the *Granja Penal de Pavon*, and further press contact was denied. One newspaper nevertheless reported that Alvarado had claimed to possess information giving the names of Guatemalan policemen who had participated in the "death and disappearance" of many Guatemalans. On the basis of these allegations, Christian Democrat leaders sent a cable to President Laugerud on April 15th urging a stay of execution until investigations into the death of Humberto Gonzalez Juarez had been concluded. On the next day Lauro Alvarado y Alvarado was executed by firing squad in the prison precinct. Though, coincidentally, condemned criminals were executed in two other prisons on the same day, it was the first time for several years that death penalties had not been commuted to long terms of imprisonment.

In the meantime, the violence continued. Though official complicity cannot be proven in every case, concerned private citizens at least have done everything possible to collect evidence that could be used for prosecution. This has included (i) reporting on the discovery of clandestine cemeteries, (ii) eye-witness accounts of abductions by security forces, detectives, men in military uniform, or the Mobile Military Police, and (iii) noting the number plates of vehicles used for abductions. This chapter analyses the background to the violence, and reproduces evidence collected by concerned people in Guatemala.

2. The Origins of Political Violence

Organised political violence first became a major national issue in the early 1970s. The governments of Castillo Armas (1954-57), Ydigoras (1958-63) and Peralta (1963-66) had all ruled by decree, facilitating curbs on individual freedoms but also paving the way for social unrest and the consequent development of a violent left-wing opposition. Under the Ydigoras government radical elements within the army staged an attempted coup; but during the Peralta regime discontented army officers formed a number of separate guerrilla organisations: MR-13, the Rebel Armed Forces (*Fuerzas Armadas Rebeldes* – FAR) and the Edgar Ibarra Revolutionary Front (*Frente Guerrillero Edgar Ibarra* – FGEI).

Left-wing political violence (directed exclusively against military and police officers, right-wing politicians, large landowners and foreign diplomats and military personnel) reached its highest point in the middle and late 1970s, and has been far less prominent in recent years. President Arana claimed to have eliminated the guerrilla movements, and until late 1976 the Laugerud government denied the existence of any organised guerrilla or 'subversive' opposition. In 1976, after a series of military operations in Quiche province, Laugerud's government again made public reference to guerrilla activity, and since then there have been a number of references in the Guatemalan press to the activities of a Guerrilla Army of the Poor (*Ejercito Guerrillero de los Pobres* – EGP) which has recently claimed responsibility for assaults on right-wing politicians and the sites of large (and multinational) enterprises. Governments have never been able entirely to eradicate armed left-wing opposition, however much military, logistic and financial support they have received from the USA for counter-insurgency programmes, and many politicians and writers have argued that guerrilla activity will never cease as long as the present social and economic injustice prevails. On the other hand, it is important not to exaggerate the extent or effect of guerrilla activity so far. To quote again from de Leon Schlotter:

Guatemala has also suffered violence from political guerrilla warfare, which most often represents marxist ideology. This phenomenon is relatively limited in comparison with the violence of the right: in force (no more than 450 men at the peak of their activity), in mobility (the mountains of the Northeast and the Western Plateau) and in time (from late 1961 to 1968, and again in 1976) ... I can tell you that in my country the guerrillas have not acted against the non-political sectors, but only against the government and the ruling sectors. Their violent action has been more discriminating than that of the fascist groups. From 1968 until the end of 1975, guerrilla warfare was virtually wiped out, so they could hardly have been responsible for the waves of terror that took place in their absence ...[9]

Guerrilla activity will continue to be a factor in Guatemalan political life if there is no scope for open political opposition. But there can be no doubt that the militarisation of society and repressive legislation (a state of siege was in force for over four years in all between 1963-71 alone) has facilitated the existence of right-wing paramilitary groups for which there can be no justification on grounds of national security.

The first of the widely publicised mass disappearances occurred in March 1966, towards the end of the Peralta regime and just before the presidential elections. 28 members of the outlawed Guatemalan Communist Party (*Partido Guatemalteco de Trabajo* – PGT) were abducted by various military patrols. In what appears to have been a coordinated assault on the PGT, some members were arrested during a clandestine meeting, others by officials from the Retalhuleu Military Base, and others by detachments of police intelligence (*Policia Judicial*). Though both civil and military authorities denied knowledge of the detentions, a young official who later defected from the military police gave an eye-witness account of how these PGT members had been assassinated in the Matamoros military barracks, and their bodies later dropped into the Pacific Ocean[10].

In 1966, the first organised anti-communist death squads began to appear. The most notorious of these, the MANO, distributed its first leaflets in June 1966, and was followed in 1967 by some 20 other similar groups[11]. Amnesty

9. Schlotter, op. cit.
10. Data taken from *La Violencia en Guatemala*, Fondo de la Cultura Popular, Mexico DF. 1969. The document is a reproduction of the denunciation made by the Guatemalan Committee for the Defence of Human Rights, November 1968.
11. AI International Briefing, op. cit.

International has reported that the MLN political party at this time declared its open support for the organisation of armed groups of civilians to fight 'subversion', and in September 1966 published a manifesto stating that "the government should not consider it strange if citizens organise to take justice into their own hands"[12]. In December of the same year, when severe counter-insurgency measures had been introduced in the provinces of Zacapa and Izabal (where the guerrillas were most active), legislation was approved commissioning large landowners and their administrators as law enforcement agents authorised to bear arms[13]. As Amnesty International has pointed out, this emergency measure was a direct contravention of the Guatemalan Constitution of 1965. Article 215 of the Constitution states that the "organising or functioning of militias other than the army of Guatemala" is a punishable offence. Furthermore, Article 398 of the Penal Code of 1973 now prescribes a penalty of from three to ten years for those who "organise, constitute or lead groups of armed men or militias that are not those of the state" as well as those who "aid or collaborate economically in the maintenance of these groups".

The 1966 presidential elections were won by Julio Cesar Mendez Montenegro, candidate of the moderate Revolutionary Party (*Partido Revolucionario* – PR), and a man who had pledged during his electoral campaign that under his government there would be no "disappearances or assaults on human dignity"[14]. The reality was tragically different. As already noted, this was the period of greatest political violence from both left and right. In 1968 US Ambassador John Gordon Mein and two US military aides were kidnapped and killed by the FAR. The two most notable kidnappings by the MANO were of Rogelia Cruz, former Miss Guatemala (mutilated and killed) and the Archbishop of Guatemala City (later released). In March 1970 the US Embassy Labour Attache, Sean Holly, was kidnapped and released shortly afterwards in exchange for abducted guerrillas whose arrest had been denied by the security forces. In April 1970 the West German Ambassador, Count Karl von Spreti, was executed by the FAR after the government refused to accede to similar demands.

The counter-insurgency campaign, particularly in Zacapa and Izabal, was ferocious. Amnesty International cites reports that between 3000-8000 Guatemalans died in the campaign headed by Colonel Arana Osorio between October 1966 and March 1968. According to many reliable reports (including *Time* magazine), it was at the instigation of the US Military Attache John Webber that counter-terror techniques were implemented by the Guatemalan army in the Izabal areas.

In 1969 a Guatemalan Committee for the Defence of Human Rights presented a document of over 200 pages denouncing the reign of terror that had existed in the country since 1966 to the Human Rights Commissions of the United Nations and Organisation of American States. The document is of vital importance in that the allegations made are not of a general nature, but specifically

12. Ibid., p.3.
13. Ibid., p.3.
14. Fondo de la Cultura Popular, op. cit. p.25.

detailed and readily investigable. Several hundred deaths or disappearances are described, and the source of information (usually daily newspapers) is always given. Places that have allegedly been used as the headquarters of the various death squads, and the places where torture or assassination have been carried out, are described with full addresses. Eye-witnesses to abductions often describe the type, colour and number plates of vehicles used. Finally, there are five full pages listing Guatemalan military, police and security officers alleged to have been directly or indirectly responsible for abduction or assassination, and a list of 22 US officers alleged to have been involved in the counter-insurgency training.

It was alleged, for example, that the MANO had its headquarters in the Central Army Barracks at Matamoros, and that another death squad, the NOA operated from the old air force base at La Aurora. Further, it alleged that threatening leaflets were distributed from military planes (one military plane, marked TG RIO, had been spotted distributing NOA leaflets on the outskirts of Guatemala City); and that abducted people were taken to the Fourth National Police Corps situated in Zone 7 of Guatemala City or to the San Francisco Convent occupied by the National Police in Zone 1. The report also named a number of places alleged to have been used as torture centres at the time of writing. And, as examples of individual cases where evidence was given by eye witnesses: (a) In February 1967, Victor Macias Mayora was dragged from his home by heavily armed men who arrived in various vehicles, among them a jeep No. P40150 (from the series allegedly used by military intelligence). His bullet-ridden corpse was found several days later. (b)In Colonia Quetzal, Escuintla, the schoolteacher Jose Arnoldo Guillo Martinez was ambushed and abducted in July 1967 in the presence of his wife, by a group of men driving car No. P38485. He never reappeared. The police claimed there was nothing they could do for "these number plates had never been sold". (c) In July 1967, the actor Carlos Enrique Quintana was abducted in a military jeep No. 712, and never reappeared. (d) In August 1967 Mateo Sermeno, administrator of Tehuantepec farm in Santa Lucia, was kidnapped by a group carrying machine-guns, in vehicle No. P 39499, a number plate from the series used by the army for their security vehicles.15

The government party itself, the PR, did not escape the right-wing violence at this time. In March 1967, in the town of Sanarate in the province of El Progreso, three local leaders and eight other members of the PR were reported to have been abducted by four plain-clothes individuals accompanied by a member of the Mobile Military Police. They were taken to the local police station, and later transferred to Guatemala City. Their corpses were discovered a few days later.

It is often argued that the PR President, Mendez Montenegro, had no control over his own security forces and had only been allowed to occupy the presidency in 1966 after striking a bargain with high-ranking military officers and US Embassy officials that he would increase the counter-insurgency drive. Statistics appear to support this. In 1967, US military and police aid to Guatemala was more than double the 1966 figure, and total funds spent by the US Military

15. Ibid.

Assistance Programme (MAP) in Guatemala between 1967-70 were over US $6,000,000 supplemented by over $11,000,000 in foreign military sales[16]. The army and military security organisations thus had an increased budget, increased power, and also increased independence from the executive under the enforcement of a state of siege. Though Colonel Arana himself, Defence Minister Arriaga Bosque and a third military leader had been sent to diplomatic exile posts in March 1968, after a political scandal when MANO's complicity in the kidnappings of Archbishop Casariego became known, President Mendez Montenegro may have lost control by 1970.

An extraordinary account of this period has been published by the then Foreign Minister, Alberto Fuentes Mohr, who was himself kidnapped by the FAR in February 1970, and then by Arana's security forces in November of the same year. In this book, *Secuestro y Prision* (Kidnap and Prison), Fuentes Mohr describes how the activities of the MANO and a new group, Eye for an Eye (*Ojo por Ojo*), increased during the last weeks of the Mendez Montenegro government. Every day and night armed men, presenting themselves as members of the security forces, moving in cars with covered number plates, claimed new victims. Mutilated bodies were found by the roadsides, with signs or leaflets identifying the death squad that had perpetrated the crime. Fuentes Mohr had an interview with the President, and mentioned the commonly held beliefs that the government security services and high-ranking military officers were behind these acts. Mendez Montenegro reportedly answered that he had no control over these groups.

Though this may have been no more than an attempt by the Foreign Minister to exculpate the PR government from these atrocities, it may be true that the civilian government had simply lost control. The same cannot be said of the Arana government (1970-74). Arana was elected on an MLN ticket, and (in contrast with Mendez Montenegro who had pledged to eradicate 'disappearances') had promised during his electoral campaign to eradicate subversion. After a few months of comparative peace, one of the worst-ever waves of violence occurred in the months after a state of siege was declared in November 1970. The *New York Times* reported in June 1971 that at least 2,000 Guatemalans were assassinated in the six months after this; and *Le Monde* weekly quoted foreign diplomats in Guatemala as estimating that for every political assassination by left-wing guerrillas, fifteen murders were committed by right-wing fanatics.[17] The situation during the whole of Arana's government was most carefully monitored by the Committee of Relatives of the Disappeared, who chronicled 15,325 cases of disappearance between 1970 and 1975, claiming that government security forces were involved in about 75% of the cases. When bodies were found, there were usually signs of severe torture and mutilation.

Statistics — vast though the numbers are — reveal only part of the picture. Equally significant is the change in the nature of the victims of political violence.

16. NACLA, *Guatemala*, p.196.
17. Quoted in NACLA, op. cit. p.203.

In the late 1960s, when the counter-insurgency operation was in full spate, the victims had tended to be either (i) known or suspected guerrillas, and their contacts, (ii) peasants and peasant communities in areas of guerrilla activity, (iii) members of the PGT, and more occasionally trade union activists. Under the Arana government few of the disappearances and assassinations were seen to bear any relation to guerrilla activity. Many trade unionists or lawyers defending peasant interests were killed at this time. In addition, a great number of students, journalists, social democrat political leaders, and above all peasants, lost their lives.

Of the thousands of peasant cases, just one will suffice as illustration. In January 1973, *El Grafico* reported that masked and armed men kidnapped Francisco Domingo Perez Cardona, Cruz Perez Velasquez and Jesus Solares Castaneda in the port of Champerico, Retalhuleu province. Their corpses were later discovered, one on a nearby hacienda in the province of Suchitepequez, the others in a mutilated state on the road to Mazatenango. Relatives addressed a letter to President Arana, stating that the vehicles from which the kidnappings were conducted belonged to the owners of neighbouring farms who wished to evict the victims from the lands where they had lived and worked for several years. A cursory reading of the Guatemalan press of the time will show innumerable similar cases. Sometimes there is reference to official complicity, when the reporter states that the group of kidnappers wore olive-green uniforms (the military dress) or were recognised as members of the Mobile Military Police. At times there are hints of direct political reasons (as peasant agitation, or party political divergences). More often no reasons are given, and the case is rapidly forgotten.

Reprisals against opposition political parties came immediately after Arana's access to power and, predictably, again at the time of the next presidential elections. At first it was the PR that suffered most, but later the Christian Democrats. As de Leon Schlotter has described it:

A third wave of violence took place during the electoral campaign from November 1973 to 3 March 1974. Its evident purpose was to limit participation in the opposition, which had gathered around the Guatemalan Christian Democrat Party in a National Opposition Front. In the following months, the violence was particularly concentrated on the party which adopted an attitude of permanent protest at the shameless disregard for the election results, which were strongly in favour of the Christian Democrats. A dozen middle-level leaders were murdered, bombs were thrown into the party headquarters and the private homes of the General Secretary and myself, and there was a flood of death warnings against party leaders . . .

The Arana government has been aplty described as the 'terrorists in power'. The strong man who had been picked for his success and ruthlessness when in charge of the 1966-68 counter-insurgency campaign in eastern Guatemala was bound to use the same tactics when in power. This meant that the right-wing terrorists closely allied to the MLN party were able to legitimise their position, and government leaders were able to make a mockery of allegations of official violence. Landowner Roberto Herrera Ibarguen, when Minister of the Interior in 1973, once declared to the press that the Death Squad (*Escuadron de la Muerte*) was a "product of communist minds".

Such was the legacy bequeathed to General Kjell Laugerud when he assumed the presidency on 1 July 1974. The police and army were riddled with corruption, and Arana's enormous personal power and support was bound to be an important factor in both. Laugerud had attained power through elections generally accepted as fraudulent, and was seen by many as the personal selection of his predecessor. Noticeably, General Leonel Vassaux Martinez, holder of the important post of Interior Minister under Arana, retained this post during the first two years of the Laugerud government. And Laugerud's Vice-President, Mario Sandoval Alarcon, was the MLN leader whose name has been most consistently linked with the MANO.

3. Violence Before and After the Earthquake

Though the violence itself has at times been subdued over the past two years, the apparatus of violence has not been dismantled. This was more than ever apparent after the February 1976 earthquake, when a new wave of political terrorism followed closely on the natural disaster. The earthquake inevitably unleashed severe social tensions, and the Laugerud government (whatever its spoken intentions) has proved either powerless or unwilling to intervene. But first it is important to see the tensions that were already developing even before the earthquake.

In November 1974 the Central American weekly newsletter *INFORPRESS* reported that kidnappings and assassinations continued as before. During that month of November the national press had recorded eleven such cases, including two women, most of the bodies showing signs of torture. In the same month an attempt was made on the life of Jose Luis Cruz Salazar, parliamentary representative for Quezaltenango province and member of the PR. Two leading members of the Christian Democrats, Danilo Barillas and Roberto Carpio Nicole, then asserted that they too had been victims of death threats and urged President Laugerud to carry out a more effective arms control policy.[18]

In 1975, Amnesty International presented to the government of Guatemala and the Organisation of American States a survey of 134 cases of political murder and disappearance documented in the press between 1 July 1974 and 31 January 1975. The survey was intended to show only the scope and character of political violence, and assumed that the actual number of victims was higher than indicated by the press reports. It was discovered that 30 of the 134 victims of political violence were members of police or military bodies, functionaries of the government or of the governing parties, businessmen and large landowners and their employees; none of the 30 were reported to have been tortured, and all but one of the 30 were killed outright by being shot in the street. The remainder were identified as peasants, students, members or leaders of opposition parties, or sus-

18. *INFORPRESS*, 21.11.1974.

pected guerrillas (21 were identified by name alone with no further information). Of these 104 cases 30 were reported shot dead, 5 reported killed in armed encounters, 69 had 'disappeared' or had been found dead after abduction; 29 of those found dead were said to carry the marks of severe torture[19].

By mid-1975 the situation began to deteriorate yet further. In May of that year the Economics Faculty at San Carlos University reported that Rector Roberto Valdeavellano, and economist Saul Osorio Paz, had both received death threats. At exactly that time, Saul Osorio was participating in a solidarity seminar organised by the Committee of Relatives of the Disappeared. It was also widely believed that the threats were due to demands made by the university board for new petroleum legislation to protect national interests against the incursions of multinational companies. Interior Minister Vassaux promised that the Rector would receive special police protection[20].

In June and July 1975 *INFORPRESS* again summarised the growing political violence in two separate articles. Every day, the magazine reported, new cases were found. The victims were mainly peasants, both men and women; although the violence occurred throughout the national territory, it was most frequent in the south-west, east and north-east of Guatemala; as often as not, the atrocities occurred in the presence of relatives or friends of the victims who gave details of the circumstances, asserting that the malefactors used vehicles of all kinds and arms of all calibres including machine-guns and hand-grenades. Although the victims were usually ordinary individuals, they were occasionally nationally known figures. On 19 July 1975 the journalist Julio Roberto Pensamiento (employed by the daily paper *La Nacion* and the radio-journal *El Independiente*) was found assassinated on a main road in the province of El Progreso. *INFORPRESS* noted that the fire-arms used were of the 9mm calibre, whose use was only authorised for the state security forces. On the very day of his death, *La Nacion* published an article by Julio Roberto Pensamiento concerning another political assassination, suggesting that the case had political overtones. On July 22nd another writer, Jose Maria Lopez Valdizon, was kidnapped and 'disappeared' in Guatemala City[21]. *INFORPRESS* also mentioned a case in June 1975, when a farmer from Nueva Concepcion in Escuintla was abducted, beaten and shot, but survived to relate the experience; he claimed that among his captors were two members of the Mobile Military Police.

In July 1975 *El Grafico* interviewed members of the Cooperative of Professional Photographers of Guatemala, who asserted that they had received written death threats from the MANO. The threatening leaflet, published in this newspaper, stated that the MANO "knew by experience that all trade union and co-operative organisations fall under the control of communist leaders who are infiltrated into them" and warned that the MANO had the power to reply to this subversion. It pointed to "30,000 peasant and clandestine graves" as evidence that they

19. AI International Briefing, op. cit. p.13-14.
20. Data from *INFORPRESS*, 2.5.1975.
21. *INFORPRESS*, 5.6.1975 and 24.7.1975.

spoke the truth.[22]

In December 1975, Axel Mijangos Farfan, employee of the Guatemala City Municipality and Vice-President of the metropolitan division of the Christian Democrat Party, was shot dead. *La Nacion* reported that he had presumably been abducted from his home, killed, and later dumped on the road to Atitlan where his body was found. In the next month, January 1976, national publicity was given to the assassination of Raiza Alina Giron, schoolteacher from the Quiche province. Her sister, who witnessed her abduction in Guatemala City, took down the number plates of the car (yellow Volkswagen P 127339), which reportedly belonged to the Detective Corps, and appealed to Interior Minister Vassaux for support. According to her own account of the interview she was told that if she had witnessed the abduction and would be able to recognise the captors, she should take precautions for her own safety.

So much for right-wing and alleged official violence under the Laugerud government. It has been difficult to pinpoint organised left-wing or guerrilla violence, for the simple reason that until very recently the authorities have always denied the existence of a guerrilla movement. Moreover, the evident factionalism among the right-wing political parties themselves now makes it impossible automatically to attribute the death of a prominent military officer or right-wing politician to a guerrilla group. But we have seen that, of the 134 *political* cases studied by Amnesty International, more than 22% of the victims were from the government, military or business sectors. The claims of the left-wing groups themselves also have to be taken into account.

On 9 June 1975 Jose Luis Arenas Barrera, a one-time MLN deputy then retired from active politics at the age of 70, was machine-gunned on his estate in Quiche province. According to witnesses of the assassination, FAR members claimed responsibility[23]. In July and August 1975 the military had carried out a brutal campaign in northern Quiche, as a result of which over 30 peasants had disappeared from the small village of Ixcan Grande. At the same time Defence Minister Romeo Lucas Garcia denied that there was any guerrilla activity, while admitting that military operations (initially termed "manoeuvres") had been carried out in Quiche.

In November 1975, *El Grafico* reported that a leaflet from the newly-formed EGP guerrilla group had reached their offices, claiming responsibility for the death of 19 military commissioners near the Honduras frontier, the death of Jose Luis Arenas Barrera in Quiche, the placing of a bomb in the offices of INTA (National Institute for Agrarian Transformation), and the death of Jose Hernandez Pinto, a landowner from Chiquimula province[24].

On November 30th Valentin Ramos was shot dead after an armed clash with military troops near Chiquimula. Government officials denied that he was associated with a guerrilla organisation, and Interior Minister Vassaux took the opportunity to repeat his denial of the existence of guerrillas, and to call the

22. *El Grafico*, 11.7.1975.
23. *INFORPRESS*, 12.6.1975.
24. *El Grafico*, 30.11.1975.

EGP a "fictitious invention". However, press reports stated that among Valentin Ramos' private papers and possessions had been found the names of several farmers, military commissioners and secret army agents who had been killed, including one person described as the second in command of the MANO in the town of Gualan. Also found were several copies of EGP pamphlets, entitled *Guerra Popular*. In December, the EGP also claimed responsibility for the placing of a bomb in the headquarters of the Sugar Growers Association (*Asociacion de Azucareros*) and the assassination of Jorge Bernal Hernandez Castellon, MLN Deputy and Representative for Chiquimula. Bernal Hernandez had been head of President Arana's bodyguard during the four years of his administration and, according to the EGP, had been responsible for many disappearances during that time (later allegations have linked Bernal Hernandez with the MANO and other right-wing death squads).

At the end of January 1976 the press reported the death of two policemen and the wounding of another after a shoot-out in two separate districts of Guatemala City with presumed guerrilla members who had allegedly been distributing 'subversive propaganda'.

It can be seen, then, that tensions were rising sharply at the time of the earthquake. Right-wing violence, often clearly with government complicity and the participation of several branches of the security forces, had continued unabated during the Arana regime and had not been stamped out by President Laugerud. Offenders were still not brought to trial, and the precipitous execution of Lauro Alvarado y Alvarado served only to increase suspicions that the new administration would not tolerate any investigation of political disappearances.

The generally accepted belief that Laugerud came to power through fraudulent elections paved the way for the resurgence of left-wing violence. In March 1975 a leading Christian Democrat politician, Danilo Barillas, created a stir with the publication of his book *Democracia Cristiana y Su Posicion ante el Ejercito de Guatemala de Hoy* (Christian Democracy and its Position on the Guatemalan Army Today) in which he suggested that the electoral path to power was closed to all those groups who did not resort to political violence. Barillas argued that no political decision was taken in Guatemala without the consent of the army, and that the electoral fraud had "again placed Guatemala in danger of a resurgence of guerrilla activities which would entail ferocious repression"[25]. Much of Barillas' predictions appear to have come true. While death squads, police and military corruption had not disappeared, they were perhaps less in evidence during 1974 and early 1975 than before. But as soon as the signs of guerrilla resurgence appeared in the Quiche province, a ferocious military offensive was launched, with scant respect for human life.

After the Earthquake
The first signs of newly proliferating violence came within days of the earthquake. In mid-February, the conservative daily paper *El Imparcial* reported that "No

25. From Danilo Barillas, quoted in *INFORPRESS*, 3.4.1975.

less than 10 looters have been killed by military patrols in Zones 5, 6 and 7 of this capital. Some of the delinquents were captured by civilian military patrols and handed over to military brigades who shot them on the spot". However both the Army and National Police denied participation in such acts. In mid-March *INFORPRESS* reported that no less than 40 persons had been assassinated between February 6th and the beginning of March. The crimes showed similar characteristics. Most of the victims were shot at point-blank range, and the hands and feet of the corpses were bound (a sign of death squad activity). An extreme case was that of Jose Gilberto Robles Garcia, who was assassinated in the intensive care department of the Roosevelt Hospital, where he had been taken after surviving an assault in which two other people died. In the words of *El Imparcial*: "He managed to survive for five days after a miraculous escape from the Death Squad; he was pointed to as the only person able to give a lead to the police investigating the assassination of at least 50 people, all with criminal records, after the earthquake of February 4th".

In the above cases the evidence all pointed to acts of vengeance against suspected common criminals by a Brazilian-style Death Squad. But politically motivated assassinations also occurred. On February 20th Rolando Andrade Pena, Director of Administrative Services at the Municipality, and leading member of the centre-left United Revolutionary Front (FUR), was assassinated in the centre of Guatemala City. Most analysts connected his death with the invasion of private land that had taken place since the earthquake, with the apparent consent of municipal officials. But it was also seen as an attack on the FUR party itself, and several other members of the same political party received death threats at this time.

On March 29th Manuel Colom Argueta, leader of the FUR and also Mayor of Guatemala City from 1970 to 1974 (when he had been a bitter opponent of the Arana government), was attacked by unknown men armed with machine-guns. Helped by his own bodyguards he was able to repel the attack and escape only slightly wounded. Colom immediately responded by addressing an open letter to President Laugerud, asserting that since his return to Guatemala one month previously his movements had been closely watched by plain clothes members of the Regional Police (*Policia Regional*), which he alleged to be a secret police force closely linked with disappearances and political assassinations. To facilitate investigations, Colom gave the names of three members of the Regional Police who had allegedly been watching him for the past month. When both the President's office and Interior Minister Vassaux denied the very existence of a Regional Police, Colom gave a press conference naming the leaders of this organisation during the last three governments as Major Rolando Archila under Mendez Montenegro, Colonel Elias Ramirez under Arana, and Colonel Ramon Quinteros and Major Byron Lima under Laugerud. He also gave fuller details of the three cars alleged to have been used for tailing him by the Regional Police: a white Toyota No 52983, a blue rental car No A 16863, and a cream coloured Volkswagen minibus No 66517. In giving these details Colom again urged the government to carry out a full investigation, and to terminate and dissolve the paramilitary forces which were "instruments of the extreme right not only fighting the people, but also threatening the institution of the State and the Army itself."[26]

Because of Colom's reputation, his case and Andrade's were given considerably more than the usual publicity in the national press. But it is an interesting comment on the relative powerlessness of judicial bodies in Guatemala that both the Executive Board of the Bar Association (*Colegio de Abogados*) and the Executive of the Law Faculty at San Carlos University could do no more than put public advertisements in the press appealing for a full judicial investigation into the assault on Colom, a public report of the results of the investigation into the death of Andrade Pena, and the intervention of the Human Rights Commission of the United Nations.

At the same time, violence was escalating throughout Guatemala. *INFORPRESS* described the situation over a ten day period at the end of March, using the national press as source material. Twenty separate incidents were mentioned altogether, involving both disappearance and assassination accompanied by torture. Some of the incidents appeared to have definite political ramifications. On March 23rd, the Secretary General of the Christian Democrat Party announced that he and all members of the party's executive had received death threats. The party also claimed that three of its affiliates, peasants from Quiche province, had been captured by the National Police Detective Corps and had disappeared. Police spokesmen denied all knowledge. On March 28th the corpse of Emilio Cardona, prominent member of the local CD party, was found in Villa Nueva; he had been beaten before death. Of the other cases, there were again eye witnesses of the abductions. For example, Judith Franco Calderon reported that on March 19th four men armed with machine-guns had abducted her 29-year-old son, Leonel Enrique Franco, using a yellow Toyota with number plates 55041; she stated that her son's captors had been from the Detective Corps of the National Police, but no news was received of his whereabouts.

So the violence continued. Countrywide the victims were predominantly peasants and trade union leaders. In Guatemala City students, teachers, professors, writers and others continued to suffer. In May an attempt was made on the lives of two leading national executive members of the Christian Democrat party, Enrique Guillen Funes and Alfonso Alonso. In early June a bomb exploded in the car of University Rector Roberto Valdeavellano, after a succession of threats had been made on his life. In June a bomb also exploded in the house of Dr Guillermo Rojas Mazariegos, San Carlos University representative on the National Reconstruction Committee, two weeks after the secretary of this Committee had denounced the death threats to which several of its members had been subjected. These threats to members of the National Reconstruction Committee after the February earthquake were usually explained by the jockeying for positions of power among the right-wing government parties themselves (while the earlier National Emergency Committee had been controlled

26. Various press reports.

by the supporters of former President Arana, the Reconstruction Committee was in the hands of more progressive officers and civilians).

In May 1976, though, came the first signs that the government might be moving against right-wing terrorist groups. As a result of police and military raids carried out after the kidnapping of Maria Olga Novella (daughter of one of the richest men in Guatemala), a number of arms and false documents were found at several properties of the Zimeri family. At a subsequent press conference, the police produced sub-machine guns, rifles, hand grenades, other explosives, also 10 sets of false number plates, and simulated uniforms of the National Police and the Mobile Military Police. *INFORPRESS* reported that the false number plates included some from Mexico and the USA, as well as Guatemala, and that one of the numbers was later found to correspond to one that had been used for the surveillance of Manuel Colom Argueta before the assault on his life in March 1976[27]. All these items were reportedly found in the private house of Elias Zimeri, in the San Antonio textile factory owned by the Zimeri family, and in their 'Las Marias' estate on the south coast. In the textile factory, police found the remains of a body subsequently identified as that of Lieutenant Waldemar Orozco, who had disappeared during the previous year. The police stated that Elias Zimeri and his son Jorge Antonio Zimeri would be accused of multiple assassinations, abductions, arms smuggling and arson. According to a report in *Prensa Libre* National Police spokesmen also insinuated that the Zimeri actions had major political ramifications, stating that "It is felt that the group run by the Zimeri family has connections with other powerful political elements. This has set off a series of speculations involving people who have participated in other governments, a point that will be clarified by the authorities"[28].

The events sparked off intensive research and speculation into the interests and political affiliations of the Zimeri family. It was found that, apart from the family's wide industrial and agricultural interests, Jorge Zimeri had in the previous year sought a patent for an 'improved automatic pistol'; and *Impacto* reported allegations that Jorge Zimeri had been involved in arms smuggling, together with the recently assassinated MLN Deputy Bernal Hernandez and also Oliverio Castaneda (MLN Congressman until his assassination in 1972)[29]. *Prensa Libre* also reported that the San Antonio textile factory had been mentioned as an operations centre of the MANO death squad several years previously.

In the course of investigations four employees of Jorge Zimeri were arrested. One of them reportedly stated that Waldemar Orozco had been abducted by Jorge Zimeri and two army lieutenants, and later assassinated within the factory; he also stated that Zimeri and these two army officers had carried out a series of abductions and assassinations over the previous years. Another of the arrested employees stated that he had been a member of Defence Minister Arriaga Bosque's security force before he commenced employment as a chauffeur with the Zimeris (Arriaga Bosque has repeatedly been named as responsible for the

27. *INFORPRESS*, 3.6.1976.
28. *Prensa Libre*, 31.5.1976.
29. *Impacto*, 30.5.1976.

assassination of the 28 PGT members in 1966).

The National Police also insinuated (apparently on the basis of testimony from one of the arrested employees) that Jorge Zimeri and the two army officers were implicated in a plot against the Laugerud government. Interior Minister Vassaux then gave a press conference denying this, and also stated that there was no criminal charge at present against Elias Zimeri (Jorge Zimeri had been out of the country for some time). He denied that the case had anything to do with the kidnapping of Maria Olga Novella, and tried to link the events with the activities of subversive guerrilla organisations (whose existence he had denied up till then). Shortly after this President Laugerud himself felt obliged to make a statement, saying that he had in no way interfered with the conduct of this case, and that "it devolves on the investigating authorities and the tribunals of justice to clarify these deeds, and to pass orders for the arrest or freedom [of the Zimeris]".

At the time of writing, the results of the investigations are unknown. *INFORPRESS* reported in mid-November 1976 that neither of the Zimeris had been arrested, but that Fernando Raul Morales Pineda (one of the two military lieutenants accused alongside Jorge Zimeri) had been condemned to four years imprisonment by a military tribunal for complicity in the crimes. But full investigations are vital. We have noted the accusations that false uniforms of both the National Police and the Mobile Military Police were found on the Zimeri property. Many Guatemalans have legitimate fears that such evidence could be used to exonerate the Mobile Military Police from other crimes, despite growing evidence that this body has been involved in a large number of abductions and assassinations in recent years. Yet top Guatemalan families may well be involved in criminal activities. Some commentators have plausibly connected the Zimeris with the intrigues of former President Arana himself[30]. The kidnapping of Maria Olga Novella, daughter of one of Guatemala's top industrialists, has been attributed to an Aranista faction. One witness alleged that Jorge Zimeri had been involved in plots to assassinate top executives from EXMIBAL (the North American multinational company involved in nickel extraction in eastern Guatemala), in order to disrupt the firm's activities and secure a contract for another (unnamed) US company. In October 1976 another top industrialist, Jorge Kong, was allegedly involved in the assassination of two civilians; at the time of writing, an intensive campaign by the father of the two victims has not so far led to his arrest.

Since the earthquake, the formation of the National Front against Violence and Repression (supported by trade union movements, students and opposition political parties) has served to give more publicity to the repression. It has not served to break it. Apart from the massive brutality against the peasants of Quiche, perhaps the widest publicity has been given to two cases where police complicity could hardly be denied. On June 1st Jose Fernando Lobo Dubon was arrested by members of police intelligence (*Policia Judicial*) together with four other students who were subsequently released and gave a full account of the

30. *Latin America*, 11.6.1976.

circumstances of the abduction. When the Ministry of the Interior persisted in denying that Lobo Dubon was in the hands of any of the police or security forces, his father addressed an open letter to President Laugerud holding him directly responsible for the activities of his security forces. The letter received wide publicity. On May 31st, plain-clothes detectives from the same police force had broken into the home of Mario Rene Castellanos, half an hour before midnight and abducted him. Almost one month later, his family likewise addressed a letter to President Laugerud, of which we quote relevant parts:

Dear President, in your hands lies the physical safety of our brother Mario Rene Castellanos de Leon, subjected to an unjust imprisonment since the night of 31 May 1976, that fateful date when nine members of the *Policia Judicial* broke down the doors of his home, beat him, and took him to a destination unknown to us in vehicles belonging to the Detective Corps (*Cuerpo de Detectivos*). Toyota Hi-Ace number 117555 and Ford Maverick number 545560. . . . your government is responsible for the life and physical well-being of Mario Rene Castellanos.[31]

The President replied to neither letter, but almost two months later the Ministry of the Interior felt forced to give a public reply to the press campaign waged by the Castellanos family. Predictably, the answer amounted to a blanket denial:

The Ministry of the Interior categorically denies that Castellanos de Leon is held in any of the detention centres, for these are public and there is control over the entries and exits of criminals to and from them. As this is a case of kidnapping which has not been solved the investigation continues open until there has been a solution to this lamentable affair which the Ministry has been the first to condemn.[32]

A new and powerful voice was added to those condemning the government in July 1976, when twelve Guatemalan Bishops referred to the violence as follows:

It is painful to think of the impunity with which lesser officials, abusing the power that they have received to serve the people, commit all kinds of arbitrary acts, often reaching criminal proportions. It is a violation of justice and law to have armed groups moving through the national territory at the service of opposed political factions, kidnapping, assassinating citizens, in a climate of permanent terror . . . Those institutions which exist to safeguard and impart justice are frequently put to the service of partisan interests. This gives the impression that justice should only be applied to the poor when they commit or are accused of criminal acts, and not to all citizens alike. The use of torture has persistently been verified and denounced . . .[33]

31. Quoted in *INFORPRESS*, 19.8.1976.
32. *INFORPRESS*, 14.10.1976.
33. *Unidos en la Esperanza*, Mensaje del Episcopado Guatemalteco, July 1976, p.23-4.

The episcopal message provoked a varied response. President Laugerud himself claimed to welcome it, urging only that the bishops should make practical recommendations to deal with the problems they had raised. Vice-President Mario Sandoval Alarcon, on the other hand, declared to the press that the bishops were exceeding their mandate by meddling in politics, and helping the subversive aims of the left wing.

4. Guerrilla Offensives

The six months from August 1976 to February 1977 again saw an extension of left wing guerrilla activities by the EGP. From the Zona Reina district of Quiche province, where they were first reported, the activities of the EGP spread to the western coastal estates and also to urban areas. In August the EGP claimed responsibility for the burning of 'El Paraiso' sugar farm on the south coast: and for the killing of a former military commissioner for the region, who was also the administrator of La Gomera market near Escuintla. One month later the burning of two more farms in the region was attributed to (though not claimed by) the EGP.

At the end of October, the EGP claimed responsibility for the killing of landowner Santiago Pezzarossi and his bodyguard. Pezzarossi owned no less than seven farms, and had been condemned by students and union leaders for his attempts to dislodge peasants who had been granted land on one of these estates under the 1952 agrarian reform law, and had remained on their allotment ever since 1954 (see Chapter IV).

In the following month of November, EGP claimed responsibility for a bomb placed in the Sheraton Hotel in Guatemala City (owned by the Kong family). Prior warning was given to the hotel before the explosion. The bomb was reportedly placed in reprisal for "the crimes committed by Jorge Kong" who was allegedly involved in the assassination of two civilians shortly beforehand but had so far escaped arrest. In the same month, the EGP destroyed ten crop-spraying planes on 'La Flora' cotton estate in the province of Escuintla. The attack was justified by the EGP on the grounds that "by uncontrolled fumigation of the southern coastal estates, the wealthy have caused the death of many workers, suffering to many poor families, and the death of many fish and domestic and farm animals"[34].

In December, an army helicopter was hijacked in the village of Xacibal, Quiche province, and burned. The crew were released unhurt. Another farm was burned in Escuintla. In the same month, 23 peasants were arrested in the Peten on accusations of supporting the guerrilla movement in Quiche. The conflict spread to urban areas, when the EGP launched an assault on the home of Claudio Gotlib Tichauer, one of the owners of a steel firm whose union members had been struggling unsuccessfully for legal recognition (see Chapter III)' Two steelworkers arrested in connection with the assault denied EGP connections.

At the beginning of 1977, the EGP claimed responsibility for arson on six

34. *INFORPRESS*, 25.11.1976.

sugar estates in the province of Escuintla. In communiques to the press, the guerrillas justified their action by the general repression in this area, and by the violations of the minimum wage regulations in the wages paid to the estate workers. The EGP also announced its involvement in the occupation of the areas mined by multinational oil companies in the Ixcan region.

The extensions of guerrilla activities — in the wake of official violence in Quiche, and so soon after the terror of the Arana government — were a sharp reminder that while guerrilla movements can be controlled by right-wing terror they cannot in the long run be eradicated by military means. The actions of the EGP have obviously been planned with great care. There has been no indiscriminate violence. Though killings have taken place, the emphasis has been against property rather than human life, in areas where the government's position has been weakest and where popular discontent has already been very great. On the sugar estates labour conditions were notoriously bad, but attempts to seek remedies through legal means had met with consistent failure. In 1976 a strike of sugar workers at the Pantaleon mill had spread to other areas, but had been declared illegal under an article of the Labour Code prohibiting stoppages during harvest time; the ringleaders of the strike had been dismissed without compensation. In the cotton-producing areas, the dangerous effects of indiscriminate aerial fumigation had long caused outrage among estate workers and neighbouring peasant families. The eviction of peasants by landowners was a burning issue in all areas. In October 1976 national labour leaders demanded an official enquiry into the partiality of the labour tribunals towards management rather than towards worker interests. In the areas of oil exploitation (another sector in which the guerrillas had struck) many critics condemned the excessive generosity of the contracts granted by government to the multinational companies.

It remains to be seen whether events will fulfil the predictions of the Christian Democrat politician Danilo Barillas, that the resurgence of guerrilla activities will herald another period of ferocious repression like that of the Arana government. There are indications that it may. At the beginning of 1977 the newly appointed Minister for Defence, General Otto Spiegeler Noriega, declared in an inaugural press conference that "subversion has existed in Guatemala for ten or fifteen years and remains at the same level today, but it is the army's concern to control it by combating and exterminating it". And shortly beforehand Vice-President Mario Sandoval Alarcon, leader of the extreme right wing, had attacked the church, the university and sectors of the national press as accomplices of "subversion". In recent months government spokesmen have equated labour demands with subversion, while labour leaders and their legal advisers have become the targets of violence (see Chapter III).

However, there are indications that sectors of the military (including President Laugerud himself) may be seeking a political, not merely a military, solution. Significantly when the guerrilla activity in Quiche hit national headlines in July and August 1976, the diehard Interior Minister General Leonel Vassaux was replaced by a civilian who announced plans for "a multidisciplinary commission to investigate the origins of violence in Guatemala". In the following months the army complemented its counter-insurgency operations with an extensive airlift to transport agricultural produce from the more isolated villages. And according to the London-based weekly political report *Latin America*, high-ranking Guatemalan officers and their US advisers are increasingly of the opinion that peasant support for rising guerrilla activity can only be countered by limited reforms including a measure of land distribution[35].

In the final analysis, few people would disagree. The tragedy for Guatemala is that, in the absence of legal remedies, this message could only be put across by violence which is liable to engender a violent backlash.

5. The Violence of a System

Apologists for the Laugerud government have argued that violence has long been endemic in Guatemala, and that it has been beyond the capacity of the present or previous administrations to bring it totally under control. Acts of violence have been attributed to subversion, to party political factionalism, and at times to sheer 'gangsterism'. The violence has frequently transcended ideological motives, as was clear in the few months after the February 1976 earthquake.

The violence is thus complex and widespread. In January 1977, *INFORPRESS* analysed the events of the past year as follows:

The violence in Guatemala, which has a marked political origin, has completely transcended this and now constitutes a phenomenon difficult to categorise. Abductions, assassinations, disappearances, assaults etc. have occurred throughout the national territory over the past year affecting – in unequal proportions – peasants, workers, students, professionals, political leaders, university authorities, the military, industrialists, policemen, government officials etc. Even the National Reconstruction Committee suffered from death threats. To these facts have to be added the tensions over land tenure, corruption and gangster practices in the police units, and a high degree of ordinary crime. But within this complex picture, one can nevertheless distinguish the guerrilla activities carried out by the EGP, and the anti-subversive activities carried out at the same time by all the state security forces. Another level of violence that can be clearly pinpointed is the gangsterism of groups linked with certain sectors of the political and economic power structure . . .[36]

In July 1974, President Kjell Laugerud inherited a police and military apparatus riddled with corruption, and closely linked with the rightist terror groups. Whatever his personal convictions, the dismantling of the repressive apparatus would have been a difficult task.

Lawyers' groups have taken public stands against the institutionalised violence, but to little effect. In the Ninth Congress of Lawyers held in Guatemala City in November 1976 a Commission for the Rule of Law and Protection of Human Rights demanded that:

(i) Government authorities dissolve the paramilitary groups and adopt the

35. *Latin America*, Political Report, 7.1.1977.
36. *INFORPRESS*, 13.1.1977.

necessary measures to prevent the participation of state security officials in illegal activities.

(ii) The executive branch of government should purify all national police forces, and dissolve the Detective Corps of the National Police, since there was also a judicial section of the police under the control of the Public Prosecutor (*Ministerio Publico*) providing greater guarantees for protection against ordinary crime.

(iii) That the decree of 27 June 1973, authorising the Mobile Military Police to act as bodyguard for private individuals should be repealed.

(iv) That the state should promote the reforms needed to produce structural changes, in order to mitigate the violence inherent in the socio-economic system of the country.

Concerned lawyers can make general demands, but are powerless to do much else. The reforms and police purges can only be carried out by a strong executive willing to accept the political consequences. And external factors, particularly the attitude of the United States government, are all-important.

Much of the responsibility for the present violence must rest with the US government, as much for its interventionist aid policies in the 1960s and 1970s as for its direct military intervention in 1954. We have seen that the US gave unprecedented military and police aid to Guatemala during the late 1960s for 'counter-insurgency' purposes. While extensive counter-insurgency training was given to military and police officers in Guatemala and Panama, over 1000 policemen received further training at the International Police Academy in Washington (which has only been closed recently, after a strong lobby within the USA accused the Pentagon of using the school for the support of dictatorships in Latin America). The US government appears to have supported, if not instigated, the formation of paramilitary civilian groups. It was in the late 1960s, when US logistical support and advice were at their highest, that the Mobile Military Police was formed specifically "to combat rural insurgency and banditry where civilian police protection was lacking". At the same time the Border Patrol (*Guardia de Hacienda*) was brought directly into the counter-insurgency apparatus. The Border Patrol when originally established in 1954 was under the control of the Treasury Department and had as its official responsibility the collection of tariffs, taxes and other government revenue. In 1967, at the height of the guerrilla offensive, it was transferred to the Ministry of the Interior responsible for internal security. The broad functions of the Border Patrol have been described in the 1970 US Government Area Handbook for Guatemala:

Patrol members, in addition, have been charged with being alert to any indication of subversive activity. They are expected to detect the entry, exit, internal movement, or other activity of domestic or alien subversive elements. They are directed to enforce all laws relating to peace and public order, as well as to act as auxiliary to the military in case of national emergency. Under the conditions of instability existing during 1968, the latter responsibilities demanded more of their time and effort than did their primary functions. The training and experience gained in raiding illegal stills proved most valuable in ferreting out guerrilla arms caches.[37]

It is these two police units, brought by US advisers into the counter-insurgency apparatus, that have been most regularly accused of abductions and assassinations in recent years.

The US government has both the political power and a moral responsibility to put pressure on its Guatemalan counterpart to dismantle the repressive apparatus. In the meantime the Laugerud administration must take full responsibility for the violence. Though President Laugerud himself has frequently condemned it, it is clear that he and his advisers will tolerate no major threat to the existing social order. When the true facts of official violence have been in danger of coming out, he and his government have chosen to conceal them. Thus the rapid execution of former police officer Lauro Alvarado in April 1975; the refusal of his party in Congress to permit the questioning of Interior Minister General Vassaux on allegations of government complicity in the violence; and his spontaneous attack on Amnesty International in May 1976 as a "front for international communism", shortly after an Amnesty delegation had left Guatemala.

International pressure must be put on the Guatemalan government to make the first serious judicial investigations. Evidence is certainly available in the form of eye-witnesses, identified cars and number plates, identified weapons, forensic examinations, secret cemeteries and much more. But an impartial investigation would almost certainly reveal complicity at the highest levels, and Guatemala does not have the democratic institutions to conduct its own Watergate.

37. *Area Handbook for Guatemala*, US Government Printing Office, 1970, p.323.

III Trade Unions and Labour Conflict

1. Introduction

In Guatemala, there are less workers organised in trade unions today than 23 years ago. Though unofficial sources in 1976 estimated that there were approximately 80,000 workers affiliated to the three major confederations, an official source in 1974 registered only 27,486 trade union members[1]. This was 1.62% of an economically active population registered in 1973 as approximately 1,700,000. Yet in 1953, shortly before the overthrow of the Arbenz government the government statistics office (*Direccion General de Estadistica*) reported that approximately 100,000 workers were organised in trade unions, out of an economically active population of just under one million (over 10%)[2].

In some ways the slow growth of trade unions over the past decade — when industrial development has been more rapid than beforehand — is even more disturbing. After the military coup of 1954, the Castillo Armas government outlawed the most prominent union federations, imprisoned labour leaders, and killed at least 200 prominent unionists within a few weeks of the coup. But controlled unionism was encouraged in the decade after that, and in July 1964 the Department of Labour Statistics registered 23,895 organised workers (about 2% of the economically active population)[3]. The percentage thus declined yet further between 1964-74.

The last few years have seen a significant resurgence of trade union activity, after President Laugerud expressed his verbal support for the freedom of labour organisation. At the same time labour organisers and union members have been confronted with violence, discriminatory legislation, and Labour Courts reputedly biased in favour of management. Since the February 1976 earthquake, which served to accentuate social tensions, the trade union organisations have united to an unprecedented degree in attempts to overcome these obstacles.

These events can only be understood in their historical perspective. Between 1944-54, the governments of Presidents Arevalo and Arbenz provided favourable conditions for labour organisation, while the enactment of Guatemala's first Labour Code in 1947 established a firm legislative basis for free trade union development. After 1954, though the Labour Code was substantially modified, the right to freedom of organisation was still theoretically guaranteed. The powerful confederations of the Arevalo-Arbenz period were dissolved, and their

1. Data taken from the annual report of the Guatemalan Institute of Social Security (IGSS), Editorial Marti, 1974.
2. Data taken from the 1950 Census, Direccion General de Estadistica; and report from the Departamento Administrativo de Trabajo, 1953.
3. Quoted in Mario Lopez Larrave, *Breve Historia del Movimiento Sindical Guatemalteco*, 1976.

leaders victimised, but they were able to reorganise under different names. The legislation itself has been inadequate, and has been rendered more so by the frequent imposition of states of siege curbing the right to strike or to organise labour meetings. But no government, however antagonistic to trade unions, has felt politically able to repeal the essence of the 1947 Labour Code, although clauses have been amended.

Control has been exercised in two major ways: first through violence and the intimidation of labour leaders and their legal advisers; secondly through the partiality of the Labour Courts which are empowered to declare the legality or illegality of any strike, and to confer legal status (*personeria juridica*) on the individual unions. When the courts have delayed their decisions, as has so often been the case, management has been able to dismiss organised workers without reprisals. The combination of these factors has at least until recently effectively prevented the resurgence of a powerful union movement.

2. History of the Guatemalan Labour Movement
Pre-1944
For a number of reasons — essentially the concentration of political and economic power in a few hands, the dependence on agricultural exports and the lack of industrial enterprise — organised labour developed comparatively late in Guatemala. Though small artisan and guild organisations had existed in the nineteenth century, it was not until 1918 that the first major federation was formed. In this year the Guatemalan Labour Federation for the Legal Protection of Work (*Federacion Obrera de Guatemala para la Proteccion Legal de Trabajo*) united many of the smaller organisations that had existed previously, and obtained affiliation to the Panamerican Labour Confederation. It obtained legal recognition in 1927. In May 1925, the Regional Labour Federation of Guatemala (*Federacion Obrera Regional de Guatemala* — FORG) was formed, under the inspiration and leadership of the Communist Party of Central America.

The first major labour conflicts occurred in the 1920s, as in so much of Latin America. Trade unions were formed not only in Guatemala City, but on the foreign-owned railways and on the vast banana estates of the United Fruit Company. In 1920 railway workers carried out their first successful strike, achieving most of their wage demands. But when they undertook a second national strike in 1924 the government intervened and imprisoned the principal leaders. In 1924 dockworkers of the United Fruit Company (UFC) undertook a 27-day strike after the denial of demands for a wage increase, reduction of the work-day to eight hours, and an end to racial discrimination against coloured workers. Troops were sent in to break the strike, a number of workers were killed; 22 labour leaders were arrested and subsequently expelled from the country[4]. Though strikes of this period were almost invariably countered by the killing or arrest of prominent labour leaders, many concessions were made. The eight-hour day was recognised, together with the acceptance of limited rights

4. Ibid., p.13.

to organise and to strike. An exception was made in the public sector, where suspension of work was classified as 'sabotage' punishable before Military Courts. In the private sector the National Labour Department (*Departamento Nacional de Trabajo*) was established in 1925 to deal with individual and collective conflicts.

From 1931-44, during the dictatorship of General Jorge Ubico, all labour gains were cancelled. Labour organisations, with the exception of mutual aid societies, were dissolved. New legislation was enacted to favour the employer. The vagrancy law of 1934 provided for forced labour on agricultural estates for all rural workers without fixed employment, small farmers having to do varying periods of labour according to the size of their smallholdings. In the words of Guatemalan labour lawyer Mario Lopez Larrave:

The words 'Unionism', 'Workers', 'Strike', 'Labour Rights' were forbidden vocabulary, and those people who dared to use them were automatically converted into Communists, enemies of the regime engaged in punishable conspiratorial activity.[5]

1944 - 1954

From 1944-54 the formation of trade unions in both urban and rural areas was actively encouraged by government. Though the Arevalo government had kept limitations on the right to organise in rural areas, the restrictions were removed by the Arbenz government in the early 1950s.

The 1947 Labour Code provided the legal basis for increased labour organisation, and for the overall protection of worker rights. It provided for fixed minimum wages according to sector, social security (for urban workers), an eight-hour work day, weekly rest days and national holidays. Individual and collective labour contracts were to be drawn up in industrial enterprises and on agricultural estates.

The Labour Code included provisions to protect workers against arbitrary dismissal, and to forestall the development of stooge unions (*sindicatos blancos*) partial to management. Article 211 stipulated that no other trade union could be formed in any enterprise if as many as 75% of the workers already belonged to another organisation. Another clause (Art 223) provided an important degree of protection for union leaders, guaranteeing that at least five members of the executive committee of any union could under no circumstances be dismissed during their term of office, or for a six-month period after expiry of office. Workers were entitled to strike if they considered there had been abuse of the collective contracts drawn up with management; but (Art 243) strikes were still declared illegal for public service employees, and also for seasonal labourers and agricultural workers on farms employing less than 500 people. Trade unions were forbidden participation in electoral or party politics (Art 226). Recognition of a labour union by the Ministry of Labour was considered automatic if the application were supported by more than 25% of the work force.

5. Ibid., p.17.

Machinery was also established to enforce the provisions of the Labour Code. A new system of Labour Inspectorates, Labour Courts and Labour Appeal Courts were set up within the jurisdiction of the Ministry of Labour and Social Welfare. The Labour Inspectorates (Art 278) were to seek out infringements of the Labour Code, to ensure that collective contracts were duly carried out, and to investigate the hygienic standards of industrial or agricultural premises. They were given a mandate to visit premises at any hour, to investigate wage records (Art 287) and to receive complaints from any employee. Labour inspectors were encouraged to settle disputes out of court wherever possible, but to take complaints to the local Labour Court if conciliation failed.

Labour Courts were to exist in each economic sector, their number and location to be determined by the Supreme Court of Justice. The judges, likewise appointed by the Supreme Court, were to be specialists in labour law (Art 289). In collective bargaining cases, the labour judges were to form Conciliation Tribunals in which both management and labour should be represented. The Labour Courts had broad rights of arbitration, but appeals could be made to the Labour Appeals Court (on which three judges presided, all specialists in labour law).

Trade unions flourished during this period, as much because of the partiality of the Labour Courts to the workers' cause, as of the articles within the Labour Code itself. In 1944 a number of guild organisations came together to form the Confederation of Guatemalan Workers (CTG) to replace the federation that existed before the Ubico dictatorship. Unions of railway and education workers had been formed in the same year. By the end of 1944 unions were established on a number of the large commercial farms, and in 1945 a new union was formed on the banana estates of the United Fruit Company.

Trade union development was most pronounced in the early 1950s. Whereas in November 1948 the CTG claimed only 60 affiliated unions, by 1951 the number had climbed to 180 with eleven provincial federations[6]. By the time of its second national congress in 1954 the CTG (now called the General Confederation of Guatemalan Workers, CGTG) could claim 500 affiliated unions with 104,000 members[7].

From 1950-54, for the only time in Guatemalan history, a massive degree of organisation also took place in the rural sector. A National Federation of Guatemalan Peasants (CNCG) was formed in 1950 and began to increase its membership significantly after the Agrarian Reform Law of 1952. A Decree Law enacted by the Arbenz government repealed one article of the 1947 Labour Code, removing the restrictions on the organisation of peasant unions. According to Guatemalan sociologist Mario Monteforte Toledo, the CNCG had no less than

6. Edwin Bishop, *The Guatemalan Labour Movement, 1944-59*, University of Wisconsin dissertation, 1959. Also Carole Snee, *Current Types of Peasant-Agricultural Worker Coalitions and their Historical Development in Guatemala*, CIDOC, Document No. 31, Mexico, 1969.
7. Mario Monteforte Toledo, *Guatemala: Monografia Sociologica*, Universidad Nacional Autonoma de Mexico, 1959, p.295.

1,700 affiliated bodies with 250,000 members by the time of the 1954 coup, organised either in rural labour unions or as peasant leagues[8].

In analysing the Guatemala trade union movement up to 1954, it is important once again to emphasise the very small degree of urban industrialisation reached at that time. The industrial census of 1946, for instance, revealed that there were only 776 industrial enterprises employing more than five workers, and only 19,447 workers altogether classified as employees in the industrial sector. The major strikes in the Arevalo-Arbenz period occurred in the large agricultural companies, in the United Fruit Company (1946 and 1948), in the *Compania Agricola de Guatemala* (1944 and 1948), in the *Finca Nacional de Concepcion* (1951). In the rural areas, peasant organisations were promoted deliberately by sectors of government, and also by the communist party. The increased politicisation of peasant workers, on top of far-reaching agrarian reform with its threat to landed wealth, precipitated the 1954 coup, and no significant rural organisation has been permitted since that time. Since 1954, the struggle for trade union freedom has been conducted primarily in the urban sector.

Post 1954

The labour movement was effectively destroyed overnight for a second time by the 1954 coup. Among the organisations dissolved by Decree Law on the grounds of their "communist inspiration" were the CGTG, the National Peasant Federation, the Railway and Education Workers Unions, the Unions of the UFC and the *Compania Agricola de Guatemala* and "all other political parties or groupings or associations that have been inspired by Arevalo-Arbencism or served the 'communist cause' "

In his book on the characteristics of the trade union movement in Guatemala from 1954-75 published in 1976, the distinguished labour lawyer Mario Lopez Larrave made the following general statements:

a. Although the process of industrialisation has accelerated, and the industrial work force has grown alongside it, trade unionism has grown only slowly and has at times remained stationary.

b. The reorganisation of professional organisations since 1954 has taken place in cities — essentially in the capital city — and was resurrected only recently in rural areas, with tremendous limitations. To protect the existing system, and to prevent the return of a militant trade unionism in rural areas, a controlled cooperative movement has been encouraged.

c. After the dissolution of some unions, and the loss of almost all leaders, trade union organisations have been reforming since 1955 with serious restrictions and impediments. These include *repression* in all its forms, ranging from mass-dismissals and blacklisting to the kidnapping, assassination and torture of leaders by paramilitary organisations; *corruption* directed from various levels

8. Monteforte Toledo, *Centro America: Subdesarrollo y Dependencia*, UNAM, Vol. 2, p.130.

(government, management and international organisations); *divisionism* supported by the very opponents of Guatemalan trade unionism, promoted either in an open fashion or discreetly through the use of stooge unions.

d. As a consequence of the factors mentioned above, professional associations are unstable. Many registered unions later disappear — inactive unions supersede the active ones — and federations and confederations are even created, grow and disappear in a very short period.

e. Many trade unions are not affiliated to any central body and have no relationship whatsoever with other unions. They are small islets concerned only with the problems of their own enterprise, a self-centred vision that has been stimulated and supported by management.

f. Because almost all the governments that have been in power since 1954 have been of the right — more or less 'ultraright' — trade unionism has had to struggle in adverse conditions, generally with administrative and judicial authorities who have either been compromised with management, or at the least timid and indifferent to workers; thus making it abundantly clear that formal trade union freedoms have only existed as the 'dead letter of the law', denied in reality.

Broadly the same conclusions were reached by the participants at the Eighth Congress on Guatemalan Law, in November 1974. In their concluding comments on labour legislation, the attendant lawyers stated that, whereas Guatemala had signed the relevant ILO covenants formally recognising the right to syndical freedom, "despite this legal recognition, the rights implied by such freedom are denied to Guatemalan workers, who are frequently abused when they attempt to exercise these rights"[9].

The reorganisation of labour unions since 1954 has taken place gradually. Adjustments to the 1947 Labour Code at first ensured that only those leaders acceptable to government attained the top posts. Those few unions which had legal recognition at the time of the coup were required to elect within a three month period new officers who would be acceptable to government or else lose their legal status[10]. By April 1955 only 23 unions had been reorganised, and only *two* of these were rural. By 1961 there were 54 unions officially registered with the Ministry of Labour and Social Welfare, and a number of other organisations within the public employee field, with functions largely comparable to those of trade unions (as teacher groups, municipal employees, road and telegraph and postal workers etc.). By this time, the Inter-American Regional Organisation of Workers (ORIT) — the western hemisphere branch of the International Confederation of Free Trade Unions — had gone to great pains to build up a non-militant union movement in Guatemala, which had considerable backing from successive military governments. When the Trade Union Council of Guatemala (*Consejo Sindical de Guatemala* — CSG, ORIT affiliated) held its Convention in 1961, it was significant that the President of Guatemala addressed the opening

9. Colegio de Abogados de Guatemala, *Octavo Congreso Juridico Guatemalteco*, Guatemala 1974.
10. Carole Snee, op. cit., p.39.

and closing sessions.

The old unions of the CGTG attempted to organise after 1954 first through the Autonomous Trade Union Federation of Guatemala (*Federacion Autonoma Sindical de Guatemala* – FASGUA). But, according to labour leader Antonio Obando Sanchez, FASGUA was directly or indirectly attacked from its inception, and all leaders persecuted[11]. Obando Sanchez claimed that leaders of the CSG, on the other hand, were bought off by offers of public posts. In 1962 a third current of trade unionism appeared, with the formation of the Christian Federation of Guatemalan Workers (*Federacion Cristiano de Trabajadores de Guatemala*) with Christian Democrat links. This organisation, later changing its name to the National Confederation of Workers (*Central Nacional de Trabaja-dores* – CNT), has come to be perhaps the strongest of the confederations. In the slightly more favourable environment under President Ydigoras in the early 1960s, the first real attempts were made to reorganise small-holding peasants, and four separate small federations were created in rural areas, though the Peasant Federation of Guatemala (*Federacion Campesina de Guatemala* – FCG) did not gain legal status until the late 1960s. The unstable situation of the new trade unionism was emphasised in 1963, when the Ydigoras government was ousted by yet another military coup. Unions were summarily disbanded in several companies (including the US-owned GINSA tyres, PINCASA paints and PROKESA sisal fabrics)[12].

In the late 1950s and the 1960s there were very few strikes, and even fewer successful ones. Since 1954 the effect of government policy was to diminish the political authority of the union movement, restricting activities to the presentation of complaints and pleadings to the Labour Courts. The exact extent to which court decisions favoured management is uncertain. Mario Monteforte Toledo has asserted that in 1955-6 the new judges of the Labour Courts adjudicated in favour of management in 90% of the 3970 cases brought before them[13]. However, the US sociologist Richard Adams has argued that when cases were brought by the labour unions before the Court of Appeals, the decision quite frequently went against management[14]. But the essential point is that whereas in the past the unions could show collective strength, they now had to rely on the presentation of individual complaints to a legislative body which was believed by the workers themselves to represent the interests of management. If court decisions went against them, workers were liable to immediate dismissal, and might be compelled to pay the costs incurred by the factory during industrial action. This in itself was a strong disincentive to industrial action, and may serve to explain the rapidly decreasing number of cases brought before the Labour Courts.

11. Antonio Obando Sanchez, *Historia del Movimiento Obrero Guatemalteco* (pamphlet), p.13.
12. Monteforte Toledo, *Centro America*, op. cit., p.132.
13. Monteforte Toledo, *Guatemala*, op. cit., p.299.
14. Richard N. Adams, *Crucifixion by Power: Essays on Guatemalan Social Structure, 1944-66*, Texas University Press 1970, p.427.

By the mid 1960s, by which time the guerrilla movement had started, labour unrest was countered by the violence of paramilitary groups. In 1967, for example, a series of reprisals were taken against the Union of Urban Busworkers (AUDEPA) which was attempting to negotiate a collective agreement through the Labour Courts. First, an attempt was made on the life of the negotiating secretary, Julio Monroy Monzon. Shortly afterwards AUDEPA's secretary general, Arnulfo Davila Albizures, was kidnapped and subsequently assassinated[15].

In 1970 Colonel Carlos Arana Osorio was elected President of Guatemala. He immediately declared a state of siege, virtually paralysing union activities. Labour organisers and union leaders suffered as much as any other sector from the violence of the paramilitary groups, who are estimated to have claimed over 15,000 lives during the four years of his presidency. Just a few examples will suffice.

In 1972 the Union of the *Compania Industrial del Atlantico, SA* (CIDASA) petitioned the Labour Courts for a renewed collective agreement. The union called a strike which was declared legal and lasted for 67 days. It was apparently the longest strike during this period. The union's general secretary, Cesar Enrique Morataya Paz, was kidnapped and 'disappeared'. The union was eventually dissolved[16]. In the same year, the union of *Alianza* busworkers brought a case before the Labour Courts. The negotiating secretary, Vicente Merida Mendoza, was kidnapped in June 1972 and likewise 'disappeared'.

No federation escaped the right-wing violence during this period. Jaime Mongo Davia, a leader of the government-supported CTF, was assassinated in December 1970. Tereso de Jesus Oliva, secretary of peasant affairs for the CTF (Confederation of Federated Workers), was killed in January 1972. Rosendo Bonilla, peasant leader of FASGUA, was kidnapped by a police unit on 17 June 1974, and is still listed as having 'disappeared'.

In this context of violence, there was little scope for union activity. Average wages in urban and rural areas remained so low that in September 1974, shortly after the end of the Arana government, the new Minister of Labour declared to Congress that 80% of wages did not even satisfy minimal nutritional requirements. However, one successful strike was carried out by the National Teachers Front (FNM) in 1973. When the strike commenced in July 1973, supported by almost all the country's 19,000 primary teachers, the entire staff of one school in Guatemala City was dismissed without compensation. The Ministry of Labour linked the stoppages to a "national subversive movement", and threatened that the dismissals would continue for as long as the stoppages lasted. When the dismissals continued and FNM leaders were imprisoned, university and secondary students joined the strike, while support was promised by the national labour confederations. The government finally capitulated, agreeing to a 24% rise in the salary of primary teachers, and the reinstatement of the dismissed teachers.

15. Lopez Larrave, op. cit., p.51.
16. Ibid., p.52.

46

3. Present Situation of the Labour Movement (1974-77)

The industrial and commercial sectors have grown rapidly in Guatemala in recent years. The population census of 1973 registered a work force of 1,547,340. Although the vast majority were still classified as agricultural (881,420), there were 212,780 in the manufacturing sector, 62,220 in construction, 113,800 in commerce and financial services, and 38,460 in transport, storage and communications[17]. This shows a significant increase over the 19,447 classified as employees in the industrial sector in 1946.

Although government statistics of February 1975 indicated that only 27,486 workers (less than 2% of the economically active population) were organised in trade unions, according to unofficial sources the number of organised workers may have been somewhat higher than this. The weekly magazine *INFORPRESS* calculated that there were approximately 85,000 workers (between 5 and 6% of the economically active population) affiliated to the three major confederations, CTF, CNT and FASGUA.

Of these three confederations, the largest is the Confederation of Federated Workers (*Central de Trabajadores Federados* – CTF). Affiliated to ORIT, it took its present name in 1970 after an amalgamation of the Confederation of Workers (*Confederacion de Trabajadores*) and the Trade Union Confederation of Guatemala (*Confederacion Sindical de Guatemala*). It has claimed a substantial membership of over 50,000 workers and in recent years has declared its support for the policies of the Laugerud government.

The National Confederation of Workers (*Central Nacional de Trabajadores* – CNT) recently claimed to have 17,000 affiliates in urban and rural unions. It is affiliated to the Latin American Workers Confederation (CLAT) and the World Confederation of Labour. CNT took its present name in 1968, and at one stage at least had close ties with Christian Democrat organisations. More recently, after strong pressure from the base, CNT has asserted its independence from Christian Democrat parties and has been largely instrumental in campaigning for the formation of a central workers body to represent the interests of all workers.

The Autonomous Trade Union Federation of Guatemala (*Federacion Autonoma Sindical de Guatemala* – FASGUA) was formed in 1955 and obtained legal status in 1956. Its leaders, some of whom were members of the now illegal Guatemalan Communist Party during the Arbenz regime, have been subject to persecution perhaps more than any other, and it is only over the past two years that FASGUA has become prominent. It is now considered to be stronger than the CNT in the rural areas.

In an electoral speech in Februrary 1974, General Kjell Laugerud had promised that full trade union freedoms would be restored under his government:

It is not only because it is established by the Constitution of the Republic, but also because it is an essential part of the democratic institutions that I propose to maintain and improve, that my government will respect trade union freedoms and the organisation of labour guilds. Trade unions are legitimate instruments

17. Direccion General de Estadistica, *Censo de Poblacion y Habitacion*, 1973.

for action on behalf of the workers' interests. My government will maintain friendly relations with unions . . .[18]

Some of these promises have been realised. Under Laugerud's presidency, more unions have been formed than hitherto, and more strikes have been declared legal. When strikes have occurred, the decision of Labour Courts have in some instances at least favoured the unions. May Day demonstrations took place in 1975 and 1976 without the violence that surrounded the one such demonstration permitted during the Arana government (over 20 wounded, and several killed).

On the other hand discriminatory practices by management (the threatening and harassment of workers, sacking of militants in an attempt to prevent unions being formed, and intimidation by members of the Mobile Military Police guarding industrial premises) appear to be as common as before. And after a period of improving relations between government and the labour sector during the first eighteen months of the Laugerud government, the situation deteriorated sharply in the aftermath of the earthquake of February 1976. Only a few days after the earthquake, workers from the AUROTEX textile factory in Guatemala City asserted that management had taken advantage of the earthquake to dismiss all those workers who had attempted to form a trade union within the factory, using as a dubious pretext for their dismissal the fact that they had not arrived for work in the days immediately following the 'quake. In the following month 150 employees of the Guatemalan affiliate of Coca Cola, *Embotelladora Guatemalteca SA*, who had been attempting since August 1975 to register a trade union and draw up a collective labour agreement with management, were likewise given notice of dismissal, this time on the grounds that they had "damaged the factory premises" and "attempted to form a subversive movement". In May 1976 dismissals of all official or unofficial unionised workers took place at the IODESA food factory in Escuintla, the Pantaleon Sugar Mill near Escuintla, and the *Transportes Reyes* bus company in Guatemala City.

In April 1976, ma qr labour confederations and a number of prominent independent unions and worker organisations came together to form the National Committee for Trade Union Unity (*Comite Nacional de Unidad Sindical — CNUS*). CNT and FASGUA were both represented; as were the Bankers Federation, the Sugar Workers Federation, the Municipal Workers Union and the National Teachers Front.

The first steps towards a new trade union unity were taken in 1973, with the formation of the National Trade Union Advisory Council (CNCS) in the difficult climate of the Arana regime. It was seen that strikes and other worker representations produced little effect since 1954, because with few exceptions they were conducted by individual unions without sufficient recourse to the media or other forms of popular support. Moreover, although individual unions and federations attempted to redress specific violations and made specific demands to protect the rights of their own workers, they did not feel strong

18. Speech quoted in *La Nacion*, 26.2.74.

enough to challenge the basic shortcomings of labour laws and their implementation.

But it was perhaps no accident that, after three years of preliminary consultations through CNCS, CNUS was officially constituted so soon after the earthquake. Social tensions arising at the same time convinced labour organisations that a more effective mouthpiece was needed to voice the legitimate demands of the urban poor. In their first major public appearance, on 1 May 1976, CNUS leaders urged the government to provide housing and adequate land for those sectors affected by the earthquake, to regulate rental costs, to prevent the profiteering of speculators in materials, and to set maximum prices for food and construction materials. They also demanded the right to work, the payment of minimum wages, swifter action by the courts in legalising unions in formation, and the elaboration of a new Labour Code in the drafting of which CNUS should be represented. In the following weeks, CNUS increased its criticism of government policy, protesting at the resurgence of organised violence.

On July 1st, in his opening speech to Congress, President Laugerud responded to criticism by pointing to union leaders as the "enemies of national reconstruction" and accusing them of "fabricating strikes to weaken national production and foster anarchy and violence". In the same month CNT General Secretary Miguel Angel Albizures was briefly detained. And in the following month of August FASGUA denounced a series of assassinations of union leaders affiliated to their own federation.

CNUS countered such accusations by the President and right-wing politicians by asserting that its own approach was a legalistic one, and that all its interventions fell within the framework of the law as exemplified by the (admittedly deficient) National Constitution and Labour Code. As *INFORPRESS* noted in its summary of the labour movement at the end of 1976, while the business sector and often the government itself persistently ascribed political motives to labour demands, the labour movement itself limited its specific demands to pay claims:

While the workers request from the business sector the satisfaction of their economic demands and limit their demonstrations to those authorised by the national constitution in labour matters, a substantial sector of management and at times the state itself use political and ideological arguments against trade unionism. These factors were particularly clear in the two most important labour conflicts of the past year, in the Coca Cola bottling factory and in the hospital strike. In the first case, when the conflict reached a crucial stage, the management asserted that the workers were not seeking to attain economic ends but to create political chaos as part of a large communist conspiracy. In the case of the hospital strike, editorials of important press organs pointed to the possible imminence of a "revolutionary strike in accordance with the designs of the great teachers of Marxist-Leninism". Government sectors likewise claimed that the strike aimed at the destruction of the fabric of society. In both cases workers obtained strong support from union, student and university sectors, which contributed to the success of their demands.[19]

19. *INFORPRESS Centroamericano*, 13.1.1977.

Examples of the legalistic approach came in two memoranda addressed to the President of the Guatemalan Supreme Court in October and December 1976, demanding a serious investigation into numerous cases of apparently biased application of labour law in Guatemala. In the first of these documents, signed by eight labour leaders, the basic shortcomings of both labour legislation and its application were carefully spelled out. The 1947 Labour Code, it was argued, had been advanced for its time, but would now be obsolete even if its provisions were respected. However, a series of Decree Laws had now replaced articles of the 1947 Code with new ones in the interests of management; and the most recent Constitution of 1965 had removed some of the most important articles for the protection of labour rights.

The slow and often corrupt administration of justice was said to be tantamount to a denial of justice. When Conciliation Tribunals delayed in reaching decisions, and sometimes even failed to meet after complaints had been lodged by workers, management took advantage of the delays to dismiss the workers in question.

The shortcomings of the labour judges were also pointed out. Although Articl 289 and 302 of the Labour Code stipulated that labour judges must have specialised training in labour law, this was rarely the case. The judges themselves were often ignorant of procedure, and no attempt had been made by the Supreme Court of Congress to remedy this.

CNUS also objected to the secrecy of proceedings. Although Art 431 of the Labour Code stated that the Supreme Court was responsible for the publication of the Acts of the Labour Courts (*Gacetas de los Tribunales de Trabajo*), these had not appeared since 1960; consequently, there was no record of biased or inadequate sentences passed by the Courts. And although the law stipulated that the hearings before the Labour Courts should be public if so requested, judges had denied a public hearing without giving reasons for this decision. Moreover, cases were not allocated on a fixed basis to any of the Labour Courts, and management had been enabled to select the Court of their own choice.

Next, CNUS described some of the discriminatory practices that tended to be used when hearings were held by the Conciliation Courts. First, management could give endless pretexts for not attending, thus delaying arbitration indefinitely. But if worker representatives failed to attend, a decision tended to be passed rapidly in favour of management. Second, innumerable reasons had been found for invalidating the testimony of a labour witness, such as an error in spelling his name. Trade unions had also been required to provide statutes and records of their meetings within an unreasonably short period; and if they failed to do so, they would lose their cases. When the decision of the courts went against management, enforcement had been unduly slow. Compensation did not have to be paid immediately, nor did dismissed workers have to be reinstated immediately. In fact, workers had frequently not been reinstated even after the court's decision had been in their favour.

Collective bargaining had not been permitted if a former collective agreement already existed between a section of workers and the management of any enterprise before a trade union had been officially constituted. When an agreement had been signed between a minority group of workers and management, this agreement had been accepted as valid by the courts.

At the end of the document, CNUS leaders made an urgent request for an audience with all members of the Supreme Court, and for the establishment of a commission of enquiry to report on the allegations contained in their own memorandum. The Supreme Court replied that the allegations were of a general nature, representing only the points of view of CNUS advisers, and that the audience and commission of enquiry were unnecessary. On 3 December 1976 CNUS addressed a second submission to the Supreme Court, describing 19 cases where the unduly slow administration of justice had led to reprisals against union members, 3 cases where a public audience had been denied, 3 cases where a court decision constituted an alleged breach of national law, 7 cases where judges had produced allegedly petty reasons for refusing to deal with petitions for collective agreements, and over 20 other cases where the over rigid interpretation of legal requirements had enabled management to dismiss workers or abolish unions within their plants. All of the examples were recent (see case studies below).

In a concluding paragraph, CNUS leaders emphasised that the cases presented in the December memorandum were only a selection, and by no means a complete picture of the repression suffered by the union movement. Moreover, in the face of management reprisals coupled with police repression, the poorly staffed CNUS had little time to produce a complete 'inventory':

During every day of the week, often at night, and during every holiday and weekend, we have to find means to defend ourselves from the tricks of management, from the repression exercised by employers and the police and military bodies of the country. Since the first interview that we held with the Supreme Court's President, in May of this year, many unions have been destroyed, leaders have been killed, and over 80 of our members have been jailed. This is why we have only now been able to give you an account of our treatment at the hands of the country's courts of justice.

In the face of a nationwide publicity campaign, Congressional deputies urged the Supreme Court to investigate the allegations made against the Labour Courts, but met with an immediate rebuff. The Supreme Court's president, Hernan Hurtado Aguilar, responded that the insinuation that the judicial branch was in any way biased was "unacceptable" to himself, and that it was beyond the competence of Congress to interfere with the judicial organs of government.

In the meantime, reprisals against the union movement continued. On 12 January 1977 CNUS issued a press release denouncing more threats to its leaders, and the existence of a "psychological war of intimidation designed to prevent the continuation of trade union unity". The secretary general of one union, Juan Manuel Alvarez Gil, was threatened with severe reprisals if he did not abandon his union activities. On 21 December 1976, one of CNT's labour organisers was injured in an allegedly deliberately provoked car accident (many union leaders, claimed CNUS, had coincidentally lost their lives in similar 'accidents').

Two months later there was another 'coincidence'. On 3 March 1977, the press department of CNT released the following statement:

Yesterday at 5.30 p.m., immediately after leaving the CNT head office, the organisation's legal advisers Enrique Torres Lezama and Martha Gloria de la Vega suffered an assault when an 'accident' was deliberately provoked by a green Jeep Willys, number plates 53054. According to eye-witnesses, the labour lawyers were driving along the left side of the ring road, when the jeep hit them ... knocking them off the road, where they finally crashed ... both are gravely injured. All these signs suggest a new offensive against active members of the CNT. As we remember with bitterness, we have a history of deliberate accidents costing the lives of leaders and supporters of the CNT ...

Three months after this came the most bitter blow of all to the trade union movement, when the labour lawyer Mario Lopez Larrave, who had been acting as honorary adviser to CNUS since its foundation, was himself machine-gunned to death outside his home on June 8th. Lopez Larrave had been prominent in both academic and labour circles, as Dean of the Law Faculty of San Carlos University from 1970-74, and founder of the university's trade union training centre during the same period, and had done perhaps more than any other individual to expose the inadequacies of labour legislation, as well as representing individual unions in some of their most important recent conflicts. His book, 'A Brief History of the Guatemalan Labour Movement', is the most authoritative and sympathetic account of the development of the Guatemalan labour movement in recent years.

After Lopez Larrave's assassination CNUS increased its public denunciations of the government, being convinced by then that this latest outrage was decisive evidence of a new wave of terror whose objective was nothing less than the total destruction of the trade union movement and its sympathisers. Shortly after his death, CNUS released a detailed report entitled 'Fascism in Guatemala: a Vast Repressive Plan against the People and the Trade Union Movement', linking the new wave of violence to Guatemala's proliferating economic problems and to a closely coordinated campaign of right-wing terrorism throughout Central America.

The document commenced by stating that Lopez Larrave's assassination should not be seen as an isolated event, but as part of a complex repressive plan that CNUS had been denouncing since the end of May. Repression had been the government's only answer to a rapid and spontaneous growth in labour organisation due to the rising cost of living and artificially low minimum wages, plus the growing landlessness in rural areas. While the cost of living increased by 77.4% between 1972 and 1977, there were only marginal increases in minimum wages (in 1977 US $1.42 per day in urban areas and $1.15 in rural areas, though the average family's minimum requirement for food alone was estimated to be $3.19 per day). In rural areas the search for new land and the fight against illegal eviction increased the need for organisation and militant action. In the face of this new militancy repressive measures had been introduced using the state apparatus of the courts, police and public administration, and an ideological smear campaign had been launched against worker movements.

The US government was accused of continuing complicity in the repression. While other recent accounts have taken at face value the human rights initiatives of President Carter, CNUS argued that the Pentagon had deliberately fostered militarism in Central America for strategic reasons, through logistical support for a United Central American Army which had sponsored the resurgence of paramilitary groups. To support its arguments CNUS pointed out: (i) the unpublicised presence of Pentagon officials in Guatemala, even after the Guatemalan government had publicly rejected any further US military aid; (ii) the continued training for soldiers of the Central American Army, in the USA and at US training centres in Panama; (iv) the coincidental reappearance of death squads in the three Central American countries (Guatemala, El Salvador and Nicaragua) which formed the Central American Army; and, (v) the CNUS also denounced the growing militarisation that had taken place under the pretext of threatened hostility from Belize, and the publication of a recent decree by the Ministry of the Interior declaring the need to strengthen the security services of the National Police, the Detective Corps and the Border Patrol as a matter of "national emergency".

In analysing the resurgence of political violence in Guatemala, CNUS inculpated not only the extreme right-wing political groups headed by Mario Sandoval Alarcon and Carlos Arana Osorio, but also the National Committee of Agricultural, Commercial, Industrial and Financial Associations (CACIF) itself:

CACIF has also devoted itself to the task of collecting funds for repressive activities ... Amongst the CACIF groups the most aggressive and reactionary is that of the agro-export sector which has for months been mounting a paramilitary operation headed by the notorious Colonel Churina, who has at his disposal a group of experts in repression living on the Escuintla estates, which has actually carried out many of the killings in the area ...

Statistically, the violence showed much the same pattern as in the previous year, though the increasing use of disfiguring torture against the victims suggested that the purpose was as much intimidation through terror as the physical elimination of political opponents:

The rhythm of assassinations shows the same tendencies as last year, but over the past month there have been signs that the purpose is to terrorise and intimidate, as the victims are found with disfigurements and physical mutilation. Among the individual cases from last May, we could cite one on Naricon Farm, San Andres Villa Seca in Retalhuleu, where two corpses were found with signs of torture, their genital organs swollen like footballs. In the area of Asuncion Mita, in Jutiapa province far away from Escuintla, two corpses were also found with inflamed testicles. 21 year old Edwin Omar Godoy was kidnapped, tortured and strangled; his eyes had been ripped out, he showed signs of beatings in several parts of the body ...

CNUS rejected the government's claims that independent groups were responsible for the violence:

We could point out that the present government claims to be above these terrorist acts, and appeals to the groups involved to solve their differences peacefully. In other words it attempts to convince the people of Guatemala that the repression and fascist terror is beneath and alien to the state. Nevertheless the facts we have already mentioned, the activities of those paramilitary groups under the 'direct control and vigilance of the National Army', the renewed arms build-up, the strengthening of the security services, all suggest the contrary . . .

The document ended on a pessimistic but challenging note. CNUS reaffirmed its independence from the political parties and the guerrilla movement, but urged its affiliates to prepare for an increase in repression. It warned against infiltration, for instance some external agencies who were "at the service of imperialism", and warned against wildcat strike action that could weaken the future position of the labour movement.

This document is significant in that, whereas the trade union movement's previous criticism has been on legal grounds, its public position is now clearly defined in the terms of a class struggle against ruthless opponents. But at the same time CNUS has been careful to deny outside influence (from the universities, politicians or foreigners) and based all its arguments on an analysis of the situation in Guatemala.

When the trade union movement first recovered strength in 1975 and 1976, the targets were first individual unionists and then the leaders of national federations. When the CNUS unions challenged the basis of the judicial system itself, the new targets for the violence were — predictably — the legal advisers. Although the worst excesses of the Arana regime appear no longer to occur, few would dispute the assertion of the leading labour lawyers from the Guatemalan Bar Association that there is still no real trade union freedom in Guatemala outside the dead letter of the law.

4. Some Case Histories (1975-76)
Introduction
This section describes just a few of the cases that have preoccupied union leaders over the past two years. The facts have been taken from press reports, or from CNUS press statements.

The cases serve to substantiate the union leaders' allegations — for instance, their claim that in Guatemala the slow administration of justice can be equivalent to a denial of justice. Reprisals have occurred not only when workers have taken strike action, but when they have attempted to work through the legal machinery to press their demands for better wages or working conditions. Attempts to negotiate collective agreements have been pre-empted by mass dismissals, even when by law the workers could expect protection from the Labour Courts. In several cases, employers have not only disregarded Court decisions, but have resorted to threats and violence in order to prevent the emergence of plant unions. Even when unions have been legally constituted, there are inadequate guarantees of legal protection for their members.

A. The INCATECU Shoe Factory

On 17 June 1975 an emergency committee of the workers of INCATECU (which as yet had no union) declared a stoppage of 372 of the factory's workers in protest against low wages (200 of the workers earned less than US $60 per month) and poor hygienic conditions. When the management refused to accede to worker demands, the Labour Courts declared a strike legal after an official from the Ministry of Labour had confirmed that the company provided inadequate conditions of work and realised substantial profits. In the meantime (according to *INFORPRESS*) an attempt was made on June 19th to kidnap the strike leader, Humberto Gonzalez. After widespread support for the INCATECU workers from CNT-affiliated unions and the legal department of San Carlos University, the Labour Courts decreed in favour of the workers and ordered management to pay the workers' wages during the time of strike, to provide medical aid for the workers' families and transport for those on night shifts. More importantly, the Courts decreed that the striking workers should have security of tenure for three months, and the strike committee for six months. According to the lawyer representing the strikers, this was the first time since the enactment of the Guatemalan Labour Code that security had been decreed for workers involved in such a conflict. In September 1975 the statutes of the new trade union (*Sindicato de Empleados de la Compania Guatemalteca INCATECU, SA*) were officially approved.

Reprisals were nevertheless taken. When the firm was again summoned before a Labour Court, after alleged violations of the agreement, union workers were dismissed, and attempts to secure their reinstatement have met with no success. According to one CNUS statement, the judge in this case has "arbitrarily and illegally accepted only the evidence presented by management, refusing to accept the evidence presented by workers".

B. 'La Elegante' Textile Factory

In March 1975 an ad-hoc committee presented credentials to the Ministry of Labour for the registration of a new union, the *Sindicato de Trabajadores de Camisas de Elegante* (SITFACE). Workers pleaded for security of tenure, while negotiating a collective agreement through the Labour Court. Employers immediately threatened dismissal, and put pressure on another group of workers to oppose the union's formation, and demand the dismissal of the union executive. In the meantime, CNT spokesmen denounced intimidatory practices of the military police within the factory premises. No Conciliation Tribunal was set up, and the union was completely destroyed.

C. Productos Rene, SA

On 3 January 1976 a group of workers from this factory (Guatemalan affiliate of the Filler's multinational group) presented a complaint against labour conditions, and demanded a collective agreement. Three weeks later, the company drew up a collective agreement with a minority group of workers in the company's confidence, to forestall the creation of a more militant union. On

January 28th, the Labour Court provisionally declared the workers' complaint groundless. On the following day they were all dismissed. Following an appeal, the Court later ordered the reinstatement of the dismissed workers while the case was still before the courts. On a further appeal by the company, the order for reinstatement was confirmed. As soon as the Court order had been complied with, and the case formally closed, all the workers involved were once again dismissed (on 7 June 1976).

D. Alimenticios Kerns

In June 1976 the executive committee of the unofficial union at the US-owned Kerns food factory asserted that no less than 120 workers had been dismissed over the previous forty days. While management reportedly claimed that the lay-offs were due to lack of raw materials, the union pointed out that only union members had suffered. The union had presented a collective agreement to management, and then brought their case to the Labour Courts when management failed to deal with it within the thirty days specified by law. The judge, on the evidence presented, decreed that a further thirty days should be allowed for direct settlement between workers and management, and no Conciliation Tribunal was set up (despite worker demands). In the intervening period, all unofficial union members were dismissed.

E. Industrias Oleaginosas de Escuintla (IODESA)

On 26 January 1976 the workers at the IODESA food factory in Escuintla petitioned the regional Labour Court for a new collective agreement. Five days later an ad hoc committee formed an unofficial union. In the following month a group of workers approached the Ministry of Labour, attempting to gain legal status for the union. Although, according to the Labour Code, authorisation of a union should take a maximum of sixty days, this authorisation was never granted. In the meantime a series of discriminatory measures was taken by management.

By March 1976 IODESA workers had suffered such intimidation that they addressed a letter to President Laugerud, demanding his official intervention and protection. The letter pointed out that on 3 February 1976 an anonymous note had been dropped into the FASGUA headquarters in Escuintla, threatening the FASGUA secretary for women's affairs who had assisted in the IODESA union's organisational work. The note, which was transcribed verbatim in the letter to the President, said: "Woman combatant for all trade unions dissolve the IODESA union to avoid conflict: anyone's death is a serious thing". When the FASGUA secretary chose to ignore the intimidation, a group of heavily armed men appeared at her home. When she was warned by neighbours of their presence, and took security measures, a second threatening note was delivered to the FASGUA office. Similar intimidation, the workers' letter continued, was also used against affiliated members and provisional directors of the union. On March 1st one trade unionist had been picked up in Escuintla and thrown into a vehicle that took the road for the neighbouring town of Santa Lucia Cotzmalguapa; he was severely beaten and left abandoned on the roadside. And the union's provisional director was attacked when opening the door of his Escuintla home and severely beaten by five individuals who subsequently fled. The letter demanded that President Laugerud open an enquiry into the atrocities carried out against the organisational committee.

In May 1976, while the workers' case was still pending before the Escuintla Labour Court, the IODESA management claimed that the factory (which had worked normally for 13 years) would have to be closed down for lack of vital materials. Management argued before the Court that the workers had a fixed annual contract, and could therefore be laid off without compensation. When management's case was rejected by the Escuintla regional Court it went to the Appeal Court (*Sala Primera de Trabajo*) in Guatemala City which, rejecting the union's request for a public hearing, authorised the dismissal of over 200 workers.

On May 24th, during the course of the proceedings, the labour leader Isaias Herrera Castillo was killed when struck by an official vehicle (belonging to the General Inspectorate of Highways). According to allegations by other trade unionists, reproduced in the Guatemala City newspaper *El Tiempo*, this was an act of culpable homicide, for the car accelerated with dimmed lights after dark into a group of workers.

The IODESA food factory in Escuintla is owned by the politically influential Kong family, one of whose members had recently been implicated in political violence (see Chapter II).

F. Textiles Aurora, SA (AUROTEX)
In October and November 1975, workers at this factory drew up a provisional collective agreement with management concerning labour conditions. Labour leaders asserted that, when this provisional contract was signed by both parties in December, the AUROTEX manager handed them a letter giving his word of honour that no worker would be dismissed before 25 April 2976. On 13 February 1976, only nine days after the earthquake that had destroyed the homes of many of the labour force, the manager and owner, Habie Mishan, suddenly gave the order for the dismissal of 120 workers. The general manager, supervisor and legal adviser appeared in the factory armed with revolvers, to ensure that the dismissals were carried out. In an open letter published soon after that, the dismissed workers stated that the alleged cause of the dismissals was that another factory owned by the same man (INTEXA textile factory) had been damaged by the earthquake, and that there would therefore be insufficient demand for the materials produced by AUROTEX. Labour leaders, on the other hand, pointed out that it was no coincidence that all the workers dismissed had been agitating for the formation of a trade union. The case was taken up by CNT and other unions, who eventually got the dismissed workers reinstated.

G. Embotelladora Guatemalteca, SA (Coca-Cola)
In August 1975 the CNT stated in a press release that the workers of this company (the Guatemalan affiliate of Coca-Cola) were attempting to form a trade union and to draw up with management a collective labour pact supported

by at least 80% of the factory's workers. In the past (warned the CNT) there had been severe repression against workers attempting to unionise, including the disappearance of a leader of the trade union committee in formation, whose body had later been found in another part of the country.

Steps to gain legal status for the trade union commenced in mid 1975 before the Labour Courts. Eight months after the presentation of these demands, the management suddenly announced that it had signed a separate labour agreement with another group of workers, giving better guarantees than those requested from the Labour Courts. Shortly after this, on 25 March 1976, 150 of the workers who had attempted to form the trade union were given notices of dismissal on the grounds that they had damaged the factory premises and had attempted to launch a subversive movement. Anticipating such dismissals, the workers concerned refused to leave the factory premises, barricading themselves within the grounds. The factory premises were invaded by detachments of the National Police and Mobile Military Police who (according to *El Grafico*) used violence to evict the workers, twelve of whom were imprisoned in the Pavon prison outside Guatemala City (one newspaper published a photo of the wounded prisoners before their removal).

In the midst of the crisis the lawyer representing the dismissed workers presented a legally attested document, signed by one of the employees who had allegedly signed the alternative collective agreement with the management. It is worth quoting at some length from this testimony:

I, Juan Bautista Zamora, acting of my own free will, hereby affirm: That I am mentioned as a delegate who signed a collective labour agreement with the Manager of the *Embotelladora Guatemalteca SA*, Julian Uriguen Zuazaga. This document I signed under pressure and in deceit, in order to keep my job. The assembly at which we were supposedly elected as delegates of a minority group of workers *never took place*, which is why I cannot give the date. *Embotelladora Guatemalteca SA* deceived all the workers who signeu this false document. The company told the workers that they must sign a blank piece of paper if they wished to receive their pay and to continue working there. With the exception of Cruz Aristides Cifuentes Maldonado, no one knew why he was signing this, and he knew even less of the collective agreement which he was supposedly support- ing. It is the truth that I did not know the contents of this agreement, nor that they intended to use it in the way they have done. I only now realise that what they intend to do to almost all the workers is immoral and illegal, and for that reason I refuse to allow myself to continue to be used in these deeds . . . I know that I am now in danger, and I therefore make the *Embotelladora Guatemalteca* and its personnel responsible for any harm suffered by myself, my family or my possessions . . .

Over the next weeks, allegations and counter-allegations by management and workers appeared in the major Guatemalan newspapers (while two of the major federations – FASGUA and CNT – and also the Council of San Carlos University published advertisements demanding that the President of the Republic should intercede on behalf of the dismissed workers). On March 31st an unprecedented degree of trade union solidarity was shown when FASGUA, CNT, FECETRAG, FETULIA, five sugar-workers unions, the unions of municipal workers of Guatemala City and Escuintla and representatives from peasant leagues, called for a general meeting to discuss the problems of the Coca-Cola workers. At the same time, the major unions decided to formalise their cooperation by forming CNUS as a first step towards forming a National Workers Confederation.

The impasse was temporarily resolved in April 1976, when approximately 50 unions were on the point of declaring a strike in solidarity with the Coca-Cola workers. The factory agreed to reinstate the 150 dismissed workers, and in the discussions held between workers and management within the Ministry of Labour, it was agreed that a collective labour agreement would be drawn up at a future date.

Two months later, there were signs that the conflict was not yet over. On June 15th two employees of the factory, who had been involved in the earlier strike, were assassinated by three unidentified men. The victims were Amado Aguilar Perez, aged 18, and Miguel Angel Garcia Paredes, aged 26. Fellow-workers insisted that the assassination was related to the earlier strike. At approximately the same time, three Coca-Cola workers were accused of killing a military policeman, and police vigilance was immediately stepped up within the Coca-Cola factory. Union leaders stated that they condemned the death of the policeman, and violence in general, that the union had nothing to do with the crime, and that the event was being used as another pretext for destroying the trade union.

At the end of September, a new crisis arose. Members of the union reported to the national press that, in a renewed attempt to destroy the trade union and boycott the collective labour agreement, the company had been subdivided into eight separate legal entities. The only real change was the name. The companies continued to use the same machinery, vehicles and personnel as before.

In their press statement, union members summarised the threats and obstacles placed in their way over the past year. They included threats, bribery, beatings, the arrest of fourteen workers, the illegal abduction of three others, and the knifing of two workers by unknown individuals.

On 12 October 1976, two more executive members of the company's newly formed union were detained by the Judicial Police. The arrests were made without warrant, but the prisoners were released shortly afterwards. The union treated it as a further act of intimidation and warned that, if the reprisals from police and management did not cease, a further general strike would be declared.

In March 1977, the Coca-Cola conflict took on bizarre proportions. During the night of March 1st (reported the press department of the CNT) two members of the firm's trade union, Angel Villeda and Oscar Zarti, survived a machine-gun assault outside the factory premises thanks to the intervention of a military police unit who (on this occasion at least) had intervened on the side of the workers and warded off the attack. The union produced an attested document of the previous month (dated February 10th) in which the same workers claimed that their lives had been threatened by some of the firm's officials. Shortly afterwards, the firm denied that the incident outside the factory premises had even taken place, and claimed that it had been fabricated in order to force the resignation of the personnel manager Eduardo Mejicano, who had been implicated in the allegations. The firm urged the government authorities to conduct legal investigations to verify that this was "... false information to twist public opinion, the sole aim of which was to maintain the agitated and uneasy climate within the factory"[20].

At the time of writing, the outcome of these allegations and counter-allegations is unknown. But it is perhaps significant that the alleged events were followed only one day later by the attempt on the life of two of CNT's legal advisers.

Embotelladora Guatemalteca, SA is the firm authorised in Guatemala to bottle for Coca-Cola Inc Corporation. US citizens are reported to have majority ownership; and the firm's president is a US lawyer, John C. Trotter, who resides only occasionally in Guatemala).

H. Transportes Reyes

In May 1976, an unofficial union from this company brought a collective agreement before the lower Labour Court. Shortly afterwards, workers reported a series of reprisals, even while their case was before the Court. While some workers were dismissed, the principal union leaders reported to the daily paper *La Tarde* that they had been threatened with death if they did not withdraw from the union.

Several months later, a Conciliation Tribunal had still not been set up. And, according to the CNUS memorandum of December 1976, "The judge has admitted all the delays and objections imaginable, which have held up the major court case for more than seven months. The union no longer exists".

I. Ingenio Pantaleon

On 18 May 1976 a general stoppage took place in the Pantaleon Sugar Mill. The trade union reported the allegedly unjust dismissal of one of its members, and the threatening attitude of members of the Mobile Military Police and armed plain-clothes policemen within the factory. The union demanded (i) The dismissal of the general manager, accused of brutality towards the labourers. (ii) Immediate reinstatement of the dismissed worker, Miguel Diaz. (iii) A general wage increase of US 40 cents per day for all workers, including seasonal workers. (iv) Payment of the minimum wage fixed by the collective agreement at $1.30 per day (they claimed that only 90 cents per day was being paid in many cases, whereas the national minimum wage for sugar workers was $1.12). (v) Respect for the collective agreement on work conditions. (vi) Withdrawal of the police and armed guards.

The strike had national significance, in that Pantaleon was the largest sugar-

20. *INFORPRESS*, 3.3.1977 and 10.3.1977.

producing mill in the country (having produced 1,200,000 *quintales* in 1975; and 1,400,000 by May 1976), and refined not only the sugar from its own farm, but from at least 100 other coastal farms. The rapidly growing sugar workers federation (*Federacion de Trabajadores Unidos de la Industria Azucarera — FETULIA*) gave support to the strike, as did CNUS; and the unrest spread to the unions on the neighbouring sugar mills of Palo Gordo and Santa Ana which likewise condemned repression against workers and disrespect for the existing collective agreements. The Labour Court declared the strike illegal, on the grounds that the law explicitly prohibits stoppages by peasant workers at harvest time or a time when the Law of Public Order has been declared (it had been in force since the February earthquake). On receiving a favourable decision from the Labour Courts, Pantaleon immediately dismissed 30 workers, including the Secretary General of the Union (ignoring the security of tenure which he theoretically held while occupying this post). Another 51 workers were subsequently dismissed. Of these 81, all but one were members of the union[21].

J. General Hospital
In June 1976 the medical and paramedical personnel of San Juan de Dios general hospital and the Roosevelt Hospital in Guatemala City declared a general strike, in protest against the appalling hygienic conditions that prevailed. When the general hospital had been badly damaged by the February earthquake, the facilities had been temporarily transferred to the Industrial Park. There had been no sign that reconstruction of the old hospital would commence.

The initial demands of the strikers were for (a) The resignation of the Minister and Vice-Minister of Public Health. (b) An immediate start to the reconstruction of the general hospital on its old site. (c) Establishment of the minimum conditions needed to guarantee the health of patients and medical personnel on the temporary site. In reply, the Minister of Health declared that the reconstruction would be a matter of urgency, that the old building would be demolished immediately and designs for the new one drawn up, and that improvements would be made on the temporary site ($500,000 were immediately made available for this). He also pledged that no reprisals would be taken against the workers who had been involved in the strike. Nevertheless two leaders of the Association of Nursing Auxiliaries (*Asociacion de Auxiliares de Enfermeria*), Luis Roberto Tovar Vasquez and David Hernandez Minas, were dismissed from their posts. The strike was called off. At the beginning of August Dr Julio Benjamin Sultan of the extreme right-wing MLN party was appointed the new Minister of Health. When he refused to reinstate the dismissed labour leaders, the hospital workers again declared a general strike.

The new Minister combated the strike by daily dismissals of members of the hospital staff, and by threatening to apply Art 430 of the Guatemalan Penal Code, under which employees of the public services who collectively abandon their charge, work or service would be punished by prison terms of from two to

---

21. Data from *INFORPRESS* 27.5.76, and from June 1976 edition of monthly CNT publication *Accion Popular*.

six years. While the MLN party promised to send in volunteer strike breakers, the unrest spread to the doctors of the Roosevelt hospital, and the personnel of the hospital of Amatitlan. Hospital workers also attacked the presence of plain clothes policemen in the Roosevelt hopsital.

The Minister of Health accused the Christian Democrat party and "agents of subversion" of provoking the strike; while the Government sent out a communique on August 16th declaring the strike illegal, and announcing its intention of prosecuting all workers who remained on strike. CNUS replied that the majority of Guatemalans died without access to adequate medical assistance; and that in some of the existing hospitals there were not even basic sanitary services. Within one week the Senior University Council, College of Doctors and Surgeons, Teachers and Executive Directorate of the University Medical Faculty, Faculty of Lawyers, Association of University Students and other organisations all declared their public support for the strike of hospital workers. When a doctor from Amatitlan hospital was sacked by the Minister of Health, it was reported that even the patients of the hospital were on the point of declaring a hunger strike in solidarity[22]. The strike was finally called off at the end of August, after the direct intervention of President Laugerud. All demands were accepted, including the reinstatement of sacked workers, the backpay of salaries and the withdrawal of the security troops from the Roosevelt hospital. The only exceptions were the nursing union leaders Hernandez and Tovar, who accepted transfer to another state insitution.

K. Esmaltes y Aceros de Centro America
After a plea for a collective agreement was presented by a group of workers to the Labour Courts, the company was summoned by the Court on 27 July 1976. Only on September 13th was a Conciliation Tribunal ordered by the Court. Several months later, it had still not been set up, as the labour judge accepted numerous pleas by management for non-attendance. On 12 December 1976 the home of one of the firm's owners, Claudio Julio Gotlib Tichauer, was raided by a guerrilla group. On the following day, two members of the unofficial union were arrested and accused of complicity in the raid. A workers' committee protested the innocence of the detained workers, claiming that illegal acts had been done by management rather than workers. Management, they claimed, had used "violence and threats" and arbitrary dismissals of unofficial union workers. Management was blamed for its illegal misuse of court proceedings, which had prevented the Conciliation Tribunal from delivering a verdict within sixty days of its establishment, as obliged by law.

L. Police Assault on CNT Headquarters
Ever since the earthquake, when the CNT and CTF both attacked the increasing number of dismissals that followed it, relations between government and the union movement were increasingly strained. In the May demonstration before the national palace, CNUS leaders demanded implementation of minimum

22. *INFORPRESS*, 26.8.76.

wages, more rapid granting of legal status to unions in formation, a new Labour Code acceptable to the union movement, and an end to the use of police and military forces (particularly the Mobile Military Police) to guard large farms and industrial premises and defend the interests of management. Moreover, labour leaders took advantage of the demonstration to condemn the increasing right-wing political violence, the increased US presence (including troops) since the earthquake, and the official US-backed support for the cooperative movement at the expense of genuine agrarian reform. In the same month more than 50 unions affiliated to CNUS were preparing a public document about labour repression and the violation of labour rights, in which heavy criticism would be launched against the Minister of Labour, Daniel Corze de la Roca, for his bias against the trade unions. In June 1976 CNUS gave a press conference at which it stated its intention to issue a writ against de la Roca in order to make a public statement about the repression of workers and peasants since 1954. Alleging that the present Labour Code was weighted heavily in the interests of management, CNUS leaders alleged that de la Roca had demonstrated his partisan interests towards management in recent conflicts.

On June 25th the National Police suddenly attacked the headquarters of the CNT, arrested two CNT members and also the leader of the Nicaraguan Workers Confederation (*Central de Trabajadores Nicaraguenses*), Donald Castillo, who was on a brief visit to Guatemala City. A warrant was issued for the arrest of Miguel Angel Albizures, CNT Secretary General, who had managed to evade arrest and slip through the back of the building. Two markedly different accounts of the attack appeared in the Guatemalan press. The police alleged that they had arrested the Nicaraguan leader with stolen jewellery, and then taken him to the CNT headquarters to seek a suitcase in which he was said to be carrying fire-arms; when they opened the door of the building, those inside rescued Castillo and also kidnapped a police agent; the police returned with reinforcements, recaptured Castillo and also arrested the Guatemalan CNT members after a brief shoot-out. This implausible version was published in several newspapers.

According to the CNT, the Guatemalan police first came to the building to arrest Castillo. When the CNT demanded to see a warrant, the police returned with reinforcements, heavily armed. Approximately 20 policemen stormed the building, shooting as they entered, and arrested Castillo, together with the Guatemalans Ismael Barrios and Adan Estrada Menchu. According to the newspaper *La Tarde* the trade unionists were severely tortured under interrogation, in an attempt to force them to admit to a robbery and name the "leaders of subversion in Guatemala"[23].

The police later asserted that a warrant had been issued for the arrest of Miguel Angel Albizures, on charges of kidnapping an Interpol agent, firing a gun, attempting to assassinate other detectives, and rescuing a prisoner. But two journalists from the Guatemala Journalists' Association, eye-witnesses of the assault, categorically denied the version given by the police. The Journalists'

23. *La Tarde*, 28.6.76.

Association joined the demands for the release of the prisoners and condemned the story used by the police to justify their actions[24].

On July 1st, in a speech before Congress, President Laugerud pointed to union leaders as the enemies of national reconstruction, "inspired by sectarian politics to declare strikes, weakening national production and creating anarchy and violence". CNUS leaders replied sardonically that their 'violence' lay in using the right to strike guaranteed to them by the Constitution of the Republic, while it was those allied with management, and the police and para-military groups, that resorted to kidnapping, brutality and assassination.

24. *La Hora*, 28.6.76.

IV Peasants and Land Conflict

1. Introduction

Statistics of land tenure in almost all Central and South American countries reveal similar patterns of injustice. A few wealthy individuals own most of the prime agricultural land, while the peasant majority occupy small (and increasingly smaller) plots on the most barren and eroded soil. Small farmers cultivate practically all of their land area, and on the large estates a substantial percentage of the land lies idle. In recent years the subsistence farmer has often been replaced by a new category — the "sub-subsistence" farmer and the ever growing landless rural proletariat. The growing poverty and landlessness is by no means unavoidable, but is often the consequence of social and economic policies which have deliberately maintained the marginal status of the peasantry in order to guarantee a cheap labour force for the large agricultural estates. In many countries landowners have turned away from traditional farming for local consumption, and placed far more emphasis on commercial crops for export. The major tropical export crops of coffee, sugar, cotton and tobacco all require a substantial seasonal labour force during harvest period. The landowner needs a rural labour force which is readily available, and willing to work for the very low wages that have traditionally been paid on Latin American plantations.

Guatemala is no exception to this pattern. Commercial farming for export has been practised since colonial days, but its degree and importance have increased greatly since the second half of the nineteenth century, and even more markedly so over the past twenty or thirty years. There has been but one major agrarian reform attempt in Guatemalan history (that of President Jacobo Arbenz in 1952), but the reform was rapidly reversed after Arbenz' overthrow in 1954, since it had threatened to destroy the basis of Guatemala's agricultural system of cheap labour and subsistence farms alongside vast estates. Since 1954 not only has the Arbenz reform been reversed, but an even greater percentage of the land than before has been devoted to commercial agriculture, while the average size of small farms in the highland provinces has decreased. Approximately 2% of landowners still hold over 60% of the land, while the number of tiny subsistence farms under one hectare (2.5 acres) has risen significantly over the past 20 years. Peasants are still being evicted from land which they or their ancestors had held for many years. Where litigation is involved the peasant, who generally has no legal protection or formal knowledge of the country's agrarian laws, has little opportunity of success against the superior legal and political armoury of the landowner.

The peasant farmer cultivates maize and black beans (the staple diet) often to the exclusion of any other crop. The large farmer has resisted legislative attempts to compel him to grow staple foods, preferring to use a small percentage of the land area and keep it open for speculative farming when the price of one crop is rising particularly high on the national or international market; moreover, large areas are normally reserved for cattle-grazing. During the 1970s, for much of which all of Central America has suffered drought conditions, the results have been particularly tragic. When the Nutrition Institute of Central America and Panama (INCAP) forecast large scale deaths through starvation, the Guatemalan Minister of Agriculture appealed for a massive programme of international food aid to stave off disaster. And at the best of times the malnutrition figures in Guatemala are extremely high, as much because of sheer lack of food as deficiencies in the diet.

In the eyes of most experts the only solution is agrarian reform. Even high officials of INCAP have stated publicly that scientific nutrition programmes are doomed to failure in the absence of such agrarian reform. An international committee of experts from CIDA (Inter-American Committee for Agricultural Development) made broadly the same recommendations after an intensive study in the early 1960s. Congresses of lawyers, churchmen, politicians, professors and trade unionists — no less than the peasant organisations themselves — have been making ever stronger demands for agrarian reform. In the meantime the ruling right-wing parties, inevitably representing the interests of landed wealth and agro-industry, have so far resisted the necessary reforms. The Arbenz reforms were in fact quite moderate by many standards. While asserting the social function of property and ordering the expropriation of unutilised or under-utilised private land, they allowed for the payment of compensation to affected landowners, and did not attack the structure of private property itself so much as its abuse.

Why was the resistance to the reforms so fanatical, and why have right-wing groups in Guatemala subsequently resorted to such ruthless violence to prevent the resurgence of those peasant organisations which continued to fight for an agrarian reform programme? Though part of the answer may lie in a genuine hatred of allegedly communist-inspired movements, an answer can also be found in the very structure of Guatemala agriculture which rests on the parasitic relationship between the wealthy landowners and the land-hungry highland peasantry who have traditionally provided their labour in conditions close to slavery. Forced labour existed until as recently as 1944, when it was constitu-tionally eradicated by the new president Juan Jose Arevalo. In more recent times repressive legislation has no longer been necessary to provide a rural labour force, because (with a rapidly growing indigenous population, and increasing parcelisation of land) highland peasants have been compelled by sheer economic necessity to supplement their incomes with seasonal labour on the estates. But small farmers who have increased their incomes through greater productivity or land acquisition have often immediately forsaken seasonal labour. Any agrarian reform which did satisfy the subsistence requirements of the highland peasantry would greatly affect the profits of large farmers. They might lose both land and access to their labour force, and would certainly incur far higher labour costs were conditions more favourable to the small farmer.

To appreciate this, one needs to look back into Guatemala's agrarian history from the colonial period onwards. A brief historical analysis will show how the Indian population, although treated from the Spanish invasion onwards as a source of potential labour, has always resisted this whenever possible and attempted to maintain a tradition of communal agricultural work. During the colonial period, Guatemalan Indians were allocated inalienable reservations, but had to perform periods of forced labour every year on the colonists' lands. After independence the Indian reservations were abolished, and the forced labour system was altered. Independence meant fundamentally an extension of large-scale private agriculture, never to the benefit of the indigenous population. When the labour supply was threatened, governments were always ready to take political and legislative measures to remedy this. In the 1940s and 1950s, when steps were taken for the first time to protect the interests of the indigenous population and the highland peasantry, they in turn were given a greater awareness of their own rights. Attempts since then to restore the pre-agrarian reform situation have predictably led to violence.

2. A History of Exploitation

Pre-1944

When Guatemala was colonised by the Spaniards in the early sixteenth century, the indigenous population was at first enslaved, forced to pay tribute, to work in mines and to work agricultural land for the benefit of the new colonists. Enslavement of the native population was formally discontinued approximately 40 years after the initial conquest, but to little effect. The Indians were confined to villages, where they still paid tribute and were forced to perform regular periods of unpaid or minimally paid labour on the estates of the nearby colonists. Small plots of common land were set aside, to satisfy their food and clothing requirements. The mixed race (*mestizo*) population were not given land of their own, and had no alternative but to work on the estates in exchange for the right to cultivate a plot of outlying land, or seek artisan work in the small towns that existed during the colonial period. By the end of the eighteenth century it was estimated by one contemporary observer that as many as one-third of the Guatemalan population were *mestizos* working either as tied labourers (*colonos*) on the large estates, or roaming from estate to estate in search of temporary employment[1].

The same writer asserted that at this time the best agricultural land was already concentrated in a few hands. Estates were used for cattle farming, hide production, and for the cultivation of some cash-crops including cacao, cochineal, dyes and sugar. Although the Spanish Crown had at first attempted to prevent

---

1. Archbishop Pedro Cortes y Larraz, *Descripcion Geografico-Moral de la Diocesis de Guatemala, 1768-70*; quoted in Severo Martinez Pelaez, *La Patria del Criollo*, Coleccion Educa, 1975.

the accumulation of agricultural wealth by private individuals, this policy appears to have been discontinued as early as 1591 when the desperate need of revenue to fight the European wars persuaded the metropolitan authorities to legalise the sale of land to all colonists who had "illegally usurped it" up to that time.

There are few detailed studies of Guatemala's social and economic history during the colonial period. Yet the most prominent colonial historian has produced ample evidence that even then the under-use of land and the surprisingly low number of large or medium landowners was a deliberate part of economic policy[2]. Labour was in relatively short supply, although land was not, and land without labour was valueless. If the number of landowners expanded, this would inevitably increase the competition for the available labour. Sale notices of land during this period always included a reference to the number of Indians on it.

For a brief period in the sixteenth century African slaves were imported into Guatemala in large numbers. They were taken mainly to the mining areas, and to the areas of intensive sugar cultivation. But by the beginning of the seventeenth century the importation of black slaves had come to a virtual standstill. Plantation owners claimed that African slaves were rebellious and difficult to control. Indian serfdom thus proved easier to handle than negro slavery. Although this slavery was not formally abolished until 1823, shortly after independence, it became an insignificant aspect of the economy as the mining sector declined in importance[3].

Independence from Spain was declared in 1821. For the majority of the population, independence had nothing to do with liberation. Although one independence faction argued for a major land redistribution and claimed that only a substantial increase in internal consumption could provide the basis for stable economic development, most of the new leaders (themselves from the wealthiest landowning sectors) argued in favour of increased agricultural production through the transfer of national land to selected private owners. Even at that time, one of the documents circulated by the defeated radical faction sounded much like a modern analysis, deploring the fact that most Indians had not even sufficient land to plant basic foodstuffs, whereas much of the land contained in the cattle farms was left untended and uncultivated. Within four years of independence new legislation had provided for the sale of untilled common land (*baldios*) to private individuals. Just over ten years later a nationwide Indian insurrection brought to power a conservative *mestizo* named Carrera, whose major political platform was the restoration of the status quo of colonial days. According to a US traveller who witnessed the insurrection at first hand, its major cause had been precisely the extortions practised on the agricultural and labouring classes since the declaration of independence[4].

The land tenure system was most radically altered towards the end of the nineteenth century. In 1871, at the time of a world-wide coffee boom, the landowning merchants of the Guatemalan Liberal Party regained political

2. Martinez Pelaez, op. cit.
3. Ibid.
4. G.W. Montgomery, *Journey to Guatemala, 1838*, Wiley and Putnam, Broadway, 1839.

power. Coffee cultivation expanded rapidly, and soon became Guatemala's principal export crop and major earner of foreign exchange. Coffee exports rose from 95 *quintales* a year in the 1850s to 113,000 in 1870, to 290,000 in 1880, 543,223 in 1890, and 846,679 in 1915[5]. To service the boom, the country's land tenure and labour institutions were again profoundly changed at the expense of the indigenous population and poor rural workers.

A law passed in 1873 again encouraged the sale of national lands, in individual lots of between 45-225 hectares, and a later law of 1894 established an upper ceiling of 675 hectares for individual lots (a law that appears to have been little heeded). Between 1870 and 1920 over one million hectares of land were sold or distributed, almost all of them to landowners, merchants and a new wave of foreign immigrants. The Liberal President Justino Rufino Barrios, who came to power in 1871, gave particular encouragement to immigrants, offering free land to all those who would promote the cultivation of rubber, coffee, cacao or sarsparilla plantations, or develop cattle-ranches. In consequence, coffee production was soon dominated by the German immigrant population. By 1913, 170 German-owned coffee farms produced 358,000 *quintales* as against 525,000 *quintales* produced on all Guatemalan-owned farms. An enclave economy arose in the northern province of Alta Verapaz, from where agricultural produce was exported directly to Germany through a small port on Lake Izabal[6].

The rise in cultivation naturally increased the demand for labour and (in the case of coffee) above all seasonal labour. Further attempts were made in the late nineteenth century to break up the communal lands, and increase the Indians' dependence on paid agricultural labour. In 1872 President Barrios ordered the Indian communities to pay rent for the common lands to which previously they had held the right of free usufruct. And it appears that the land parcels given to foreign immigrants were taken not only from the public domain, but also through the alienation of Indian common land made possible by the Indians' confusion over the registration requirements instituted in 1877[7].

Repressive legislation was still needed to force the Indians to move to the estates. Landowners were encouraged to indebt the Indian population, advancing credit on the condition that they should contract to work for a fixed period of time on the estates. In 1877 a legal framework for debt-peonage was provided through the enactment of a notorious new law, the Ruling for Labourers (*Reglamento de Jornaleros*). This Ruling ordered the peasant to carry a workbook recording his debts, and enabled the local authorities to arrest any defaulters. Rural workers were classified in three separate categories: first the labourers (*colonos*) who would contract to work for four years at a time on an estate in exchange for the right to cultivate subsistence crops on a plot within the estate, but even after the expiry of the four years had to pay off all debts incurred before he was legally entitled to leave the estate; second those who had

5. One *quintal* = approximately 100lbs.
6. Sandford Mosk, *Coffee Economy of Guatemala, 1850-1918*, Inter-American Economic Affairs, 1955, Vol. 9, No. 3, pp.6-20.
7. Quoted in Carole Snee, *Current Types of Peasant-Agricultural Worker Coalitions and their Historical Development in Guatemala*, CIDOC Document No. 31, Mexico, 1969.

received no land, but had nevertheless incurred debts which they had to work off before leaving; and third those who had incurred no debts, but signed short-term contracts which they were obliged to fulfil. While the new law had been passed to regulate the employment of workers by the various landowners, political bosses (*Jefes Politicos*) were installed in all areas of the country to control freedom of movement. Their powers included the issuance of passports to Indians who wished to travel from one part of the country to another.

Similar policies were pursued by all governments up to 1944. President Lisandro Barillas (1885-92) ordered that *all* lands should be recognised by private title, a demand that proved disastrous for the indigenous communities who had never registered their land, and quite probably knew none of the legal requirements for registration. According to one source the government took away large tracts from the communal lands during this period on the grounds that they were uncultivated, although it had been traditional practice to leave part of the cornfields (*milpa*) uncultivated to allow for soil recuperation[8]. The same government began a rudimentary colonisation programme, transferring Indians from their traditional lands to the unhealthy, hitherto unexploited land of the Pacific coast[9].

At the beginning of the twentieth century the US presence was first seriously felt through the cultivation of a new export crop, bananas. In 1901 banana cultivators were granted tax exemption for exports. In 1906 the US-owned United Fruit Company signed its first contract, receiving a grant of 69,000 hectares of prime agricultural land in exchange for a guarantee that it would construct a national railroad[10]. Unlike coffee, banana cultivation did not require a large seasonal labour force, but a regular work force resident on the estate. But the capitalisation of the banana industry was from the beginning far greater than for any other export crop, requiring large-scale irrigation and the control of railroad and port facilities to guarantee swift and regular transportation.

In other areas, the Liberal era brought some progress. In 1906 the sale of agricultural workers was prohibited, and in 1923 all Central American Republics signed an agreement to bring forced labour to an end. But under President Jorge Ubico (1931-44), further measures bordering on forced labour were enacted to support the advocates of private enterprise at the expense of the Guatemalan indigenous peasantry. In a further attempt to consolidate the institution of private property, a Decree of 1931 stipulated that common land should be split up among individual peasants, in lots ranging from 3 to 8 hectares. A Decree of 1936 accelerated the sale of national land in far larger lots, this time not to the benefit of the peasantry. In a decade characterised by political patronage, huge tracts were reportedly distributed to favoured military officers. Though debt-bondage was officially abolished in 1933, it was replaced by an equally oppressive

8. Thomas and Marjorie Melville, *Guatemala – Another Vietnam?*, Penguin Books, 1971, p.36.
9. Ibid.
10. NACLA, *Guatemala*, p.19.

Vagrancy Law enacted in the following year. The law's title was an outrageous misnomer in that not only landless peasants but also those with small plots (and few peasants by now had more than that) were ordered to provide regular work on the estates. Those people owning from 10-64 *cuerdas* of land (approximately 1-6.5 acres), were forced to give 100 days of wage labour annually on the estates, those owning less than 10 *cuerdas*, or no land, had to give 150 days per year. All peasants had to carry a notebook in which the farm manager noted the number of days worked. At the end of the year those who had not fulfilled the minimum requirement could be imprisoned under the terms of the law, or forced to make up the deficit by work on the roads. A further law stipulated that all Guatemalans would have to pay a fixed sum of money, or give up to thirty days per year for public works such as road construction — and this over and above the virtual forced labour on the estates.

1944-54. The Era of Reform

Until the overthrow of the Dictator Ubico in 1944 Guatemala was still very much a feudal society, with social reforms long overdue. For the rural community the most important events after 1944 were first the passing of the Labour Code of 1947, second the Agrarian Reform of 1952, and third the rapidity of organisation of rural workers and peasant leagues after 1950, which for the first time gave the peasant farmer a voice in national affairs. Government institutions were also created to back up the Agrarian Reform with extensive credit and technical aid programmes. Attempts were also made between 1945 and 1950 to build up and strengthen a cooperative movement, though far less emphasis was given to this after the 1952 Agrarian Reform. But the reforms, much publicised though they were and have subsequently been, only marginally affected the structure of private property. During both the Arevalo and Arbenz governments it was often national lands that were distributed to the peasantry — particularly the national lands that had been granted in lots of up to 400 hectares by President Ubico to his more favoured generals, and also some German-owned lands that had been expropriated by the state after the declaration of war against Germany.

Under the government of Juan Jose Arevalo (1945-50) the new Constitution of 1945 created an important precedent by affirming that property had a social function: "Private property may be expropriated, with prior compensation, in order to satisfy a public need that has been legally proved." The vagrancy laws were abolished, and attempts were made to redefine the legal basis of land ownership to favour the marginalised Indian population. The Law of Supplementary Ownership (*Ley de Titulacion Supletoria*) passed immediately after Arevalo's access to power, ordered the registration of all lands according to ownership, category and use, and (in the words of one author) "was intended to make legal all quasi-ownership titles of the poor, especially Indians"[11]. Under the new law the legal basis of land-tenure should be the proven use of land, rather

11. Melville, op. cit., p.46.

than the dubious titles that had been produced by new land owners over the past century. The 1947 Labour Code (*Codigo de Trabajo*) provided for labour contracts, minimum wages in all sectors, and the free right to organise and to strike. There was still some discrimination against the rural sector, for at first unionisation was only permitted on the large estates employing more than 500 workers.

In December 1949 a Law of Forced Rental (*Ley de Arrendamiento Forzoso*) was enacted, enabling the landless proletariat or those with sub-subsistence plots of less than one hectare to request lots for rental in writing or verbally from the large landowner. If an excessive rent were demanded (this could not legally be more than 10% of the total value of the expected harvest) then the peasant could request an audience with the municipal authorities who would have to adjudicate immediately[12]. Many rural sociologists have argued that this latter law had very limited effect, for it only hit the medium landowners rather than large-scale ones who relied on tied labourers.

In an attempt to improve the situation of the small farmer, the Department of Cooperative Development (*Departamento de Fomento Cooperativo*) was established in August 1945. It began its activities with the formation of 21 credit agencies throughout Guatemala, and the encouragement of credit cooperatives under close state control. The programme appears to have met with little success:

Seventeen such societies were eventually established but the results were economically disastrous. Great quantities of funds were distributed through the cooperatives between 1946 and 1948, but very little of it returned. The cooperative members appeared to be interested in little other than obtaining credit, and their continued low levels of productivity prevented them from repaying the loans ...[13]

The credit programme was discontinued in 1949, and more emphasis placed on the education and development of independent cooperatives.

Under President Arbenz (1950-54), the 1952 Agrarian Reform Law provided an unprecedented threat to private property; and the new rural organisations now threatened to become the most powerful political force in the country. The hundreds of peasant leagues, now formed not only on the large estates but also among the small farmers, provided the organised pressure needed to give teeth to the Agrarian Reform Law.

The Reform Law itself, Decree 900, passed through Congress in June 1952. Important articles provided for the liquidation of feudal systems, the abolition of all types of servitude (in that all labour must be adequately remunerated), the nationalisation of expropriated lands, and subsequent allotment to the landless in usufruct or rental. Expropriated lands would be given out as private property in lots not exceeding 25 *manzanas* (42.5 acres). Government would pay compensa-

12. Azurdia Alfaro, Morales Urrutia, *Recopilacion de las Leyes de Guatemala,* Tipografia Nacional.
13. Snee, op. cit., pp.24-5.

tion with 25 year bonds at 3% interest; and land value would be assessed in accordance with tax declarations up to May 1952. The law called for expropriation of uncultivated properties exceeding 10 *caballerias* (223.8 acres) and of cultivated properties exceeding six *caballerias* (671.4 acres). The National Agrarian Department (*Departamento Agrario Nacional* –DAN) was created as the administrative organ for carrying out the reform. DAN was responsible directly to the President's office, bypassing the country's legislative bodies. Regional Agrarian Commissions were created in each province, composed of five members appointed on the recommendation of DAN, the provincial governor, the Agricultural Association (landowners) and the General Confederation of Labour and National Peasants Union. Moreover, in each farm or small village where land might be eligible for expropriation, an Agrarian Committee was set up. One member of each Agrarian Committee was to be appointed by the provincial governor and the municipal government, and three by the local peasant union or labour union on the estate[14]. The Agrarian Committees were to make an inventory of affected lands, draw up registers of the land recipients and peasant organisations, and deal with the individual land requests. To provide credit for the new allotments, the National Agrarian Bank was created in June 1953.

Under the terms of this law, rural organisation was clearly supported from above, as an indispensable part of the agrarian reform process. Union leaders and political activists, in particular members of the Communist Party, travelled around the country in order to inform peasant communities of their rights under the new legislation, and enrol them into new Agrarian Committees.

According to statistics presented by CIDA, 1002 plantations were affected by the law between January 1953 and the overthrow of Arbenz in June 1954. Though the total area of the land affected was 1,091,073 hectares (2,694,950 acres), only just over half of this land was actually expropriated private land, with US $8,345,545 paid as compensation[15]. 107 national farms were also distributed, 61 of them in small lots of from 5-25 hectares (depending on whether or not the land was cultivated), and 46 farms as cooperatives[16]. Of the expropriation of private lands, one student has estimated that this represented only 16.3% of the total idle cultivable land in private hands[17]. Another observation was that 40% of the expropriated land was from farms owned by twenty-three people in lots of over 4,000 hectares each.

Allegations that the reforms were communist-inspired multiplied when a substantial portion of the United Fruit Company's unused land was expropriated. Though compensation was paid by the government the company claimed that the land was grossly undervalued.

If the US-backed invasion had not taken place in 1954, one can only hazard a guess at what the final outcome of the reform would have been. The process of

14. Ibid., pp.26-7.
15. Comite Inter-Americano de Desarrollo Agrario (CIDA), *Tenencia de la Tierra y Desarrollo Socio-Economico del Sector Agricola, Guatemala*, Washington, 1965, p.41.
16. Melville, op. cit., p.77.
17. Melville, op. cit., p.76.

land distribution was certainly being accelerated at that time. But it is important to realise that the numerical extent of the distribution in favour of the small farmer under the Arbenz law, was in fact less than the adjudications to large farmers under two successive governments at the turn of the century. Under President Lisandro Barillas, 509,433 hectares, and under President Manuel Estrada Cabrera 697,087 hectares, had been adjudicated to foreign settlers, foreign companies such as the UFC, and commercial farmers[18]. However, as we have seen before, any far-reaching change in the land-tenure and labour system would have had a social and economic multiplier effect. With more land for small farmers and thus less seasonal labour, with non-partisan agrarian and labour courts enforcing the enactment of labour laws and regulated labour contracts, with political power and freedom of organisation and expression to the peasant masses, the fabric of Guatemalan society would have been irrevocably altered.

Post 1954

Rural organisation has never been permitted to recover since 1954. The first military presidents, Castillo Armas, Ydigoras and Peralta simply made rural unions illegal. More recently, since the mid 1960s, paramilitary death squads and detachments of the Guatemalan army have resorted to systematic intimidation or killing of the promoters of rural organisations. The great majority of victims have been ordinary peasant farmers. Legislation since 1954 has been designed to consolidate the position of large commercial farmers, and also to open the way for substantial new investment and mineral extraction by the powerful multinational companies that now dominate the Guatemalan economy. Although colonisation schemes have been encouraged — all too often, alas, for the benefit of the military and land speculators — and deliberate attempts have been made in recent years to stimulate the cooperative movement, life for the average peasant is still akin to that of the pre-1944 or even colonial days. For many people land parcels are in fact smaller than in 1950. Hundreds of thousands of indigenous peasants continue to undergo annual seasonal migration to the coastal farms, in what has been described by the English sociologist Andrew Pearse as "the most spectacular inequality and injustice to be found anywhere in the world, and where the family living on estate labour frequently earns a wage which is one hundredth part of the income which the proprietor family draws from the estate"[19].

The Agrarian Committees were immediately disbanded after 1954, together with the peasant leagues which had integrated them. A Department of Agrarian Affairs was established, to whom all landlords who had had property expropriated had the right to appeal. In almost all cases, decisions were favourable to the landlords, and peasants who had occupied the land for a brief period were summarily removed. According to estimates given by the General Directorate of Agrarian Affairs to the CIDA investigators in the mid 1960s, only 0.4% of the beneficiaries of the agrarian reform had retained their land by January 1956,

18. Alfonso Guerra Borges, *Geografia Economica de Guatemala*, San Carlos University Publications, 1969, p.272.
19. Andrew Pearse, *The Latin American Peasant*, Frank Cass, London, 1975, pp.95-6.

whereas the other 99.6% had been reinstated as labourers or renters of private, national or municipal land, or transferred to the newly created areas of rural development (see below). Many peasants were evicted by force, while others fled. One report produced in 1954 listed over 150 peasants murdered in several different areas.

Decree 57 of 1954 ordered that all national lands allotted to peasants during the previous administration should revert to the patrimony of the state (though all national lands allotted to large landowners and foreigners during the earlier liberal administrations presumably remained in private hands). Another Decree of 1954, No 170, permitted landowners to re-establish the system of *colonato* (the 'feudal' arrangement by which they could drastically reduce wages by making small land plots available for subsistence farming, to ensure a low-cost labour supply). Land reform was replaced by a slow process of colonisation, the aims of which were first expounded in Decree 559 of 1956, more commonly known as the Agrarian Statute (*Estatuto Agrario*). New areas of rural development were to be opened up on unused national lands, while unused private land could in theory still be expropriated "after all legal formalities have been completed and all resources have been exhausted, the State being required to pay for the land in cash immediately or in under ten years". For renters and sharecroppers, rents were fixed at 6% of the value of production for land without irrigation, and an unlimited amount for irrigated land. In these conditions, favourable to the land-owning sector, only 160,000 hectares were distributed over the next eight years, including the national lands in the development areas and urban allotments. The Agrarian Statute was replaced in 1961 by an optimistically titled Law of Agrarian Transformation (*Ley de Transformacion Agraria*), to be administered by a new organisation, the Institute of Agrarian Transformation (INTA). The overall policies, though, were much the same as before: to continue the allocation to landless peasants of family-size farms in the areas of rural development; to give individual allotments from the national land or private land acquired by government; and to establish new communal farms in the national lands whose topography would not permit partition into separate lots. In fact, as later became clear, virtually none of the national lands were given to landless peasants. Out of 78 farms distributed during the Ydigoras government, 16 were returned to their former German owners, while the remainder were given to government agencies or public bodies.

One area of Guatemala that had remained almost completely untouched up to this time was the Peten, the vast jungle area of North Eastern Guatemala comprising 32% of the national territory. The Institute for the Development of the Peten (FYDEP) was created in the early 1960s, and had embarked on its first coordinated colonisation programme by the end of 1964. Again, the hopes of the small peasantry were to be rapidly dispelled. The Director stated that the area was mainly good for cattle-farming, and that 125 farms of 22.5 *caballerias* (62,470 acres) each would be created with this intent[20]. It was later announced

20. Melville, op. cit., p.187.

in 1965 that a US-backed colonisation plan would be commenced in the Peten area (330,000 hectares in all being devoted to cattle farming, and 260,000 hectares for small-scale agriculture). There have been scandals ever since over partisan granting of land in the area. It has been observed that many of Guatemala's biggest landowners were quick to stake a claim there in the early days, and that even foreign businessmen obtained the maximum-sized lots of over 800 hectares in Santa Ana area near the centre of road construction[21]. As recently as August 1975 a major scandal erupted when FYDEP published in the national press a list of people who would receive titles in the Peten area. The first problem was that official reports elsewhere had stated that 344 titles were to be given out, whereas only 245 appeared in the FYDEP list. Secondly, among the beneficiaries was the Congress Secretary and Deputy of the ruling party, Ernesto Castellanos Manzanero, and other officials or ex-officials. According to a report put out by the radio-newspaper *Independiente* both the Minister of Agriculture Fausto David Rubio and the Minister of the Interior Leonel Vassaux Martinez were among the beneficiaries[22]. The crisis was tempered shortly afterwards, when the President revoked the adjudication of the titles and created a new organisation, the National Institute for Development Administration (INAD) to assist FYDEP in drawing up a new development plan for the area. According to a joint INAD-FYDEP report brought out immediately after that, 27.4% of the adjudicated Peten land was reportedly farmed by organised peasant groups; whereas only 2.35% was held by cattle-farming enterprises. On the other hand, 750 of the families engaged in cattle-farming (on the larger plots) had received titles to the land in the course of 1975, while none of the peasant groups held legal title[23].

Apart from the Peten distributions, there has been very little allocation of land over the past decade. Between 1967-70 a total of 6,000 families received micro-parcels, whereas 138,000 families had benefited from the Arbenz Agrarian Reform. From 1970 to 1974 President Arana used land distribution only as an electoral gambit, as when parcels were allocated in the very area that had seen a peasant insurrection shortly beforehand, in which small farmers in the Jalapa district had claimed that their own cornfields were being usurped by a group of large landowners:

Fifteen days before the Presidential elections, the Arana government announced that it would grant 62 property titles to peasants from the province of San Marcos, on the grounds of a national farm. It only gave out 625 hectares. At the same time it carried out a propaganda exercise, announcing that it would purchase the land in Sansirisay, province of Progreso, the place where the peasants of Jalapa had clashed with the military with tragic results, the death of a large number of the peasants themselves and the subsequent assassination of the lawyer who had been giving them legal advice[24].

21. Melville, op. cit., p.245.
22. Reported in *INFORPRESS Centroamerica*, 14.8.1975.
23. *INFORPRESS*, 28.8.1975.
24. Carlos Figueroa Ibarra, *El Proletariado Rural en el Agro Guatemalteco*, San Carlos University Publications, 1976, p.90.

While land allocation was rare, the illegal eviction of peasants appears still to have been disturbingly common practice throughout the 1960s and 1970s. The Melvilles in 'Guatemala — Another Vietnam?' cite a number of typical cases:

a . In January 1967 sixty families in Jacaltenango (Huehuetenango) complained that they were being expelled from communal lands by the Mayor so that he could share these lands with two other large landowners. The peasants declared that they had no money to hire lawyers to defend their claims.

b. On 16 May 1967 the Indians of Cahaboncito in Alta Verapaz claimed that Oscar Lemus had stolen land that they had owned for over a hundred years, the burial place of their ancestors. They stated that he had done so by means of a fraudulent bill of sale.

c. On 8 October 1969 a family with fifteen members had to abandon its home in Chiquimula because the military commissioner in the area claimed that the land belonged to him, and he threatened them with death if they did not pack up and leave. He had already shot and wounded one nineteen-year-old son.

Innumerable other cases are described in the Melvilles' book, all taken from the reports of the Guatemala City press. At times the orders were given by INTA, at other times by the municipal authorities or landowners backed by the military or police forces. In many of the cases cited, the evicted peasants claimed they had received their plots under the Arbenz Agrarian Reform, or even under the 1956 Agrarian Statute.

By the 1970s, Guatemalan landowners had to some extent moved away from coffee cultivation and diversified into other commercial crops. Annual sugar production rose from approximately 500,000 *quintales* in the 1920s, to over 4,000,000 *quintales* in the 1970s. (The loss of the Cuban sugar supply for the United States after the revolution more or less guaranteed a stable market for sugar.) Vast areas of the coastal lowlands have been brought into sugar production, providing some regular employment but again accentuating the need for surplus seasonal labour. (A study of the work force on one sugar estate near Santa Lucia Cotzmalguapa in 1966 showed that 1698 seasonal workers were employed in that year, as against 251 permanent agricultural labourers.) The growth of cotton cultivation has likewise increased the labour requirements. A study by the Planning and Statistical Department of the Guatemalan Ministry of Labour in 1972 found that 21 cotton farms employed no less than 41,556 seasonal labourers, and 2,350 permanent labourers[25].

Developments since 1954 have only served to reinforce the essential features of the Guatemalan rural economy, the need for a peasant population that has land for some subsistence requirements, but not enough to satisfy them all. The political force of the peasantry was first broken by legislation against organisation, and then by systematic repression of selected peasant leaders, after a degree of rural organisation had been permitted. As peasants, and particularly

25. Ibid., p.103.

Indian peasants, have lost their organisational strength, they have again become the victims of exploitation at the hands of municipal authorities, landowners and corporations.

3. The Present Situation

Land Tenure and Standards of Living

For statistics of land tenure, census figures of 1950 and 1964 are available. As land distribution apart from the Peten has been insignificant since 1964 (taking into account the reversal of the 1954 reforms), these serve as a fairly reliable indicator. In the western part of the country, the average farm's land area went down from 10 *manzanas* (17 acres) in 1950 to 8 *manzanas* (13.6 acres) in 1964, whereas (more significantly), the number of farms under one hectare (2.5 acres) rose from 74,259 units in 1950 to 85,083 units in 1964. The area of land per rural inhabitant went down from 1.3 hectares in 1950 to 0.8 in 1964, but in some of the provinces where the smallest *minifundios* (sub-subsistence land-holdings) predominated the area was far less (0.3 hectares per inhabitant in Totonicapan: 0.4 in Solola)[26]. At the upper end of the scale, there were signs of some changes, although a tiny percentage of the farmers still owned the vast majority of the land. The 1950 Census listed 2.1% as holding 72% of the land: whereas in the 1964 Census the top 2% held 62% (some critics have claimed that this is not a sign of redistribution of privately owned land, but only of the partial distribution — to politicians among others — of national lands). At the bottom end of the scale there are now estimated to be 400,000 *minifundista* (owner of a *minifundio*) families, and 175,000 landless adult rural workers.

The population has increased dramatically. Whereas the 1950 Census recorded 2,790,868 inhabitants in Guatemala, by 1973 this had increased to over 5,600,000; over 60% were classified as rural, and over 40% of these as Indian. To balance this, food production would need to have risen by over 100%. Though efforts have been made to stimulate food production in recent years (a substantial portion of the AID programme in 1974 provided credit and technical assistance to the rapidly rising cooperative movement), the basic grain deficit has often remained critical. In 1952 national maize production was registered at 10,711,000 *quintales*. When it dropped to 9,400,000 *quintales* in 1953 and below that in 1954, opponents of the Arbenz regime blamed the Agrarian Reform for the decline, though production dropped even more markedly to under 8,000,000 *quintales* in the years after his overthrow. In 1965-6, total corn production was only 88,826 metric tons — still under 9,000,000 *quintales*[27]. At the beginning of 1973 the government announced that it would have to import vast quantities of corn — over 10,000 metric tons were imported in one week — blaming the deficit on illegal hoarding and exportation. In February 1974, when

26. Figueroa Ibarra, op. cit., p.79.
27. Statistics from Fletcher, Graber, Merrill and Thorbecke, *Guatemala's Economic Development: the Role of Agriculture*, Iowa State University Press, p.43.

further large quantities had to be imported, the extent of the deficit was so great that a bill was presented before Congress — hotly disputed by landowners in the Chamber of Agriculture — attempting to force all farmers with more than 100 *manzanas* to cultivate basic grains on at least 7% of their land[28].

There were further drastic shortages in 1974. In January 1975, Guatemala was forced to import maize, beans and rice from the USA and Colombia at greatly inflated prices (paying US $4,263,600 for the purchase of 112,200 *quintales* of corn and beans from the USA). In November 1975 the process was repeated. According to reports from the Ministry of Agriculture anticipated corn production would be 18,900,000 *quintales* in 1976, for a demand calculated at 20,200,000; bean production would be 1,400,000 *quintales*, for a demand of 2,000,000; wheat would be 700,000 *quintales*, for a demand of 1,200,000; sorghum would be 1,000,000 *quintales*, for a demand of 1,200,000. Rice production alone equalled and exceeded the demand[29]. The Minister of Agriculture later reported that basic grains would be imported, to the value of US $7,000,000, to offset the deficit and guarantee price stabilisation[30].

At an FAO meeting in 1974, the Guatemalan Minister of Agriculture had predicted that the grain deficit for the Central American region as a whole in 1975 would be no less than 1,500,000 tons, and that the region would have to purchase over $100,000,000 worth of basic grains if widespread starvation were to be averted. To back up the statement, the director of the Central America Nutrition Institute (INCAP) likewise predicted that up to 75,000 people would die of malnutrition in 1975[31]. *INFORPRESS* produced statistics to show that from 1960-72 the region depended more and more on grain imports, and that the "coefficient of grain sufficiency had declined 5.2% during this period"[32].

It is no surprise that the grain shortage was seen as a regional problem, for the whole of Central America has witnessed a process of massive land-grabbing and consequent rural proletarianisation over the last century. In El Salvador, where the problems are most acute, illegal expropriation of land had become so significant since the late nineteenth-century coffee boom that the vast majority of the country's best agricultural lands are reputed to be held by only fourteen families; further concentration of land has taken place under the more recent cotton boom, large cotton farms now occupying almost all of the Salvadorean coastal littoral. A similar process has taken place in Nicaragua under the years of the Somoza dictatorships, under which the landless rural labour force in cotton and sugar areas is over 1000% greater in some parts than 20 years ago[33]. And in all Central American countries the institutional problems are similar: the lack of credit and a marketing outlet for the small farmer. We noted earlier that the

28. *El Imparcial,* 18.2. 1974.
29. *La Tarde,* 3.11.1975.
30. *El Grafico,* 4.11.1975.
31. Quoted in *INFORPRESS*, 31.7.1975.
32. Ibid.
33. Unpublished paper on rural proletarianisation in western Nicaragua, by Edmundo Jarquin Calderon.

Arbenz government attempted to provide financial credit for the small farmer to back up the Agrarian Reform, through the creation of a national agrarian bank. The National Bank for Agricultural Development (*Banco Nacional de Desarrollo Agricola* — BANDESA) is certainly still in existence in Guatemala, but benefits for the small farmer are minimal. According to the bank's statistics for loans granted between 1964-73, 41.4% of credits went to cotton farmers, 36.3% to coffee farmers, 8.8% to sugar farmers, and only a pitiful 2.9% to the producers of corn, beans and rice (generally speaking, the *minifundistas*)[34]. In 1967 of US $47,000,000 of aid to the agricultural sector, $9,000,000 went into cattle ranching[35].

'With no state credit, and no credit from the commercial banks who are inevitably unwilling to lend to the small farmer for lack of collateral guarantee, the *minifundista* has to resort to the small local money-lender, or 'hoarder' (*acaparador*) as he tends to be known in local jargon. The hoarder has two sources of quick profit. He either lends at an extortionate interest rate, charging as much as 10% per month, or buys a percentage of the future harvest at considerable discount. The results for the peasant family can be disastrous. If their total production is little more than their subsistence requirement, they are forced to buy produce back in the later months of scarcity, when the price of the basic grains may have risen by up to 10 times or more. As prices always fluctuate according to demand, the price is exorbitantly high in a bad year.

The Guatemalan National Institute for the Commercialisation of Agriculture (INDECA) exists to collect, store and market the country's grain produce, to stabilise prices, and to calculate demands and deficits. It has had little effect to date, both because its storage facilities are minimal (less than 2,000,000 *quintales* altogether in 1976), and because it controls only a small percentage of national basic grain produce. *El Grafico* reports a typical situation in 1974, when 640 tons of grain were exported to the USA in June, and 5,000 tons had to be re-imported back from the USA at inflated prices in October after large farmers had ignored the order to devote part of their lands to grain cultivation[36]. Moreover, although INDECA will accept grains at a fixed price when brought to its storage silos, it has limited facilities to collect from the small farmer.

Though it is true that Guatemalan agriculture has been adversely affected in recent years by periodic droughts and the rocketing international price of fertilisers, hunger and starvation in the country should arouse not the sympathy but the outrage of the world at large. There is land enough in the country to produce the food, and a more than ample workforce to cultivate the land. But discriminatory policies of credit and technical aid, plus the appalling land distribution and the reluctance of landed farmers to cultivate produce for internal consumption, have guaranteed that the majority of the population remain in a situation close to starvation. Remarkably, during one of the most acute

34. *Boletin de Estadisticas Bancarias*, Banco de Guatemala 1973; quoted by Figueroa Ibarra, op. cit.
35. III Congreso de Economistas, Guatemala; quoted by Figueroa Ibarra, op. cit.
36. *El Grafico*, 8.7.1974.

recent food shortages, one right-wing lobbyist argued before Congress that the deficits were due to large scale urban migration, and proposed that the migrants should be ordered back to their land. To what land, one might ask? In August 1976, a leading doctor from INCAP gave his own point of view, bluntly stating that 80% of all Guatemalan children under five years now suffered from malnutrition, that the causes were political, social and economic, and that the only solution to this kind of poverty was a dynamic, swift and efficient agrarian reform[37].

Child malnutrition and infant mortality are by far the worst in Central America. The infant mortality rate (number of children who die under one year old per 1000 live births) according to UN statistics for 1970-75 is disturbingly high in comparison with other countries in the region: 83 in Guatemala as against 45 in Nicaragua and 37 in Honduras. Over half of all deaths in any given year are still of children under five years of age, despite endless nutritional aid programmes mounted by foreign governments or charitable organisations. The inflationary process has hit the Guatemalan peasant as hard as anyone, and virtually prevented him from regularly supplementing the basic diet of corn and beans. Apart from the rapid rise in such items as fertiliser prices, fruit and vegetables, cereals and meat were estimated to have risen by as much as 56% in 1974 alone [38].

Commercial Farming: The Plight of Seasonal Labourers

In 1975 the value of the major agricultural export products was US $400,000,000. Broken down, this represented coffee, $158,000,000, sugar, $116,000,000, cotton, $77,000,000, bananas, $30,000,000, and meat, $19,000,000. If the present coffee prices were maintained on the international market, it was estimated in June 1976 that coffee exports alone might bring in over $450,000,000 in the coming year.

Not surprisingly, the owners of these commercial estates live like feudal barons. The writers of the CIDA report of 1965 visited twelve of these farms, and studied the life styles of the owners:

Of the 12 large farms we studied on the western coast, we found that eleven of the owners lived in the capital city: six were in commerce, two were industrialists: one a financial investor: one an ex-military man and one a doctor. The one exception worked full-time in agriculture, in an agricultural limited company. The cases of these large landowners typified the tendency pattern in this kind of exploitation, characterised by absentee owners dedicated to other activities, who leave their farms in the hands of administrators. The majority of this group of landowners had received further and university education, and many of them had studied abroad; they often sent their children to be educated in the USA or Europe. As regards their life style, we could see that it is quite high and luxurious. They have all the commodities of modern life. Their

37. Quoted in *El Grafico*, August 1976.
38. Quoted by Figueroa Ibarra, op. cit., p.92. The study had been carried out by the Instituto de Investigaciones Economicas del Occidente, Quezaltenango.

members try to maintain an aristocratic colonial life style, while they also try to idealise and imitate North American standards. They have a large house, with several servants, luxury cars . . . At the same time they visit social centres characterised by their high cost, and keep up with fashion . . . The people in this landowning group frequently travel abroad, and they have a marked tendency to internationalise their social relations . . . We also observed that, like investors in any Latin American country, the wealthiest of them invest in land as a form of speculation[39].

The CIDA report might have added that since 1954 they have had a tendency to hold high government positions, and to dominate the right-wing parties in the official government coalitions. Ex-President Carlos Arana is one of the largest landowners in the east of the country, and his Foreign Minister, Roberto Herrera Ibarguen, among the foremost sugar farmers in the west. The life style of these people is incredible by any standards. Many own not one but several farms, and also keep farms in the western highlands to provide a guaranteed labour pool. Tied labourers are permitted to work small plots on their highland farms, on the condition that they perform the low-cost and compulsory seasonal labour at harvest time.

The Herrera family in particular has amassed a remarkable degree of wealth over the past century, by combining commercial farming with financial speculation, aided by the important political posts held by members of the family in successive generations. It is worth analysing in some detail the fortunes of this one extended Guatemalan family. Manuel Maria Herrera, a successful coffee farmer during the first years of the coffee boom, was a founder member of Guatemala's International Bank in 1877, and became one of the country's leading commercial figures. He was also Minister of Development under President Justino Rufino Barrios, and was himself involved in the enactment of the forced labour legislation of the Ruling for Labourers (*Reglamento de Jornaleros*). In the next generation Carlos Herrera Luna served briefly as President of the Republic (April 1920-December 1921) and also purchased large farms in both coastal and highland areas. Near Escuintla he bought the El Baul estate (which, after subsequent additional purchases of neighbouring farms, came to cover over 13,000 acres), San Juan Perdido estate (over 2300 acres) and El Carmen (over 400 acres). Among other estates purchased by him in the highlands was Canajal near San Martin Jilotepeque (over 7000 acres). These combined estates were later registered as the property of *Herrera Hermanos* (Herrera Brothers) which before its dissolution in 1970 was registered as the legal owner of no less than 108 separate farms, many of them of substantial size. The properties were widely spread, in the six provinces of Escuintla, Chimaltenango, Guatemala, Huehuetenango, Quiche and Sacatepequez. After the dissolution of *Herrera Hermanos,* seven members of the Herrera family became the registered owners of a new company, *Compania Agricola e Industrial El Baul SA*, which in 1973 included 42 other farms in addition to El Baul (one of the largest sugar estates in

39. CIDA, op. cit., pp.79-80.

Escuintla province). By this time the family, which had originally built its wealth on coffee over a century ago, had diversified its interests. Though coffee and cattle farming were included, the main concern of the company was now the "cultivation, refining and commercialisation of sugar and its by-products".

The highland estates had been purchased by earlier generations to provide a stable labour supply, at a time when seasonal labour was still in great demand. Although the need for a private supply has now become less acute, interviews carried out in two Herrera estates in 1976 (Rosario Canajal, of 7,800 acres, and San Antonio Sinache, of 3,600 acres) revealed that farm tenants were still allocated parcels of land in exchange for fixed periods of seasonal labour in the family's commercial farms. From Canajal, for example, they would have to do 36 days work on San Vicente Osuna coffee farm in the summer months, and 36 days on El Baul sugar estate during the winter.

It is impossible to calculate the total number of permanent or seasonal labourers on these estates. Many — perhaps the majority — work without contracts; whereas some come down from the highlands for periods of from two to three months, others may only remain for a week or so. In 1972 the Planning Department of the Ministry of Labour reported a total of 43,289 permanent workers and 177,115 seasonal workers on 887 commercial farms. 153,814 were on coffee farms, and only 3335 (1149 permanent and 2186 migratory) on the sugar estates. But a US sociologist who studied the seasonal migration to coffee farms in the mid 1960s estimated that 237,000 peasants went to the coffee farms alone during the most intensive period of 1965-6[40]. Recent studies have indicated that the present number of seasonal workers migrating to the west coast is — at the very least — well over 200,000, with over 60,000 from each of the northern provinces of Huehuetenango and San Marcos, and over 30,000 from Quiche. As these figures do not take into account the migratory flow to the coffee farms in Alta Verapaz, one can be more or less certain that well over 50% of Guatemala's *minifundistas* are forced to undertake seasonal labour at one time or another during the year.

If conditions and pay were adequate, it could be argued that there is nothing wrong with such a system. In fact, the transport and labour conditions are so appalling, and the recruitment methods of dubious legitimacy, that the system has recently been compared to one of slavery[41]. Under prevailing conditions it is no surprise that until comparatively recently brute force was needed to compel the indigenous peasantry to leave their farms. Social historian Severo Martinez Pelaez, among others, has described the situation during the Ubico regime, when Indians were chained together as they were marched through villages on the way to estates. In the 1960s, US sociologist Lester Schmid found that many farmers with less than one hectare needed to spend little more than 50 work days per year on their own land, and worked an average of 107 days per year each on the estates. But Indians would rather have any form of activity, artisan work or

40. IDESAC, *Los Minifundios en Guatemala*, 1971, p.113.
41. Presented in a paper of the Anti-Slavery Society of the UK, before the Joint Working Group on Slavery, United Nations Human Rights Commission, Geneva, August 1976.

occasional labour at home, than the arduous trip to the west coast, where they were more than likely to contract disease, where they were frequently cheated of their wages, where they arrived in trucks into which they had been herded like cattle, and upon arrival were housed in vast open huts (*galeras*), with up to 150 people in each hut, and no sanitation. Horror stories are frequent enough. Sociologist Humberto Flores Alvarado has described one case in 1964. Over 100 peasants were crammed into the back of a transport lorry in Santa Cruz de Quiche in which the exhaust pipes had been wrongly fitted; by the end of the trip, six people had died from the poison fumes, the lorry driver refusing to interrupt his trip on the news of each death; the driver, bodyguard of a powerful landowner, was not even prosecuted for the deaths (we have been unable to check the truth of the story, but have no reason to disbelieve it)[42]. And the Melvilles have cited a case in the following year, 1965, when the army went into some villages in the province of San Marcos and rounded up peasants at gun point to work on the cotton plantations. According to the newspaper *El Imparcial*, the Army was also used in two other provinces to secure labourers, apparently under orders from the provincial governors acting at the request of the Minister of the Interior who had himself been subject to pressure by the National Cotton Council[43].

But for the most part, such force is now unnecessary. For a long time now the landowners have been using a middleman, known as the 'contractor' (*contratista* or *habilitador*) to hire workers in advance, by advancing cash at the times of greatest food shortage, thus forcing them to pay off their debts on the estates. A typical situation has been carefully documented in a study of one village in Huehuetenango, San Ildefonso Ixtahuacan, written by Richard Appelbaum and actually published by the Guatemalan Ministry of Education in 1967. It was found that the number of seasonal migrants had increased from approximately 1500 in the mid 1950s to twice that amount in the mid 1960s. No one earning more than US $100 went down to the coast. In the year 1964-5 about 2900 people went down altogether, contracted by one of the 16 contractors working in the village (one of these contractors alone, who owned the only transport in the area, was responsible for hiring over 1000 workers). Of the others, four were *mestizos* owning shops where alcohol was sold (it was extremely rare to find Indians acting as contractors). Some of them also acted as the authorised moneylenders (*prestamistas*), who lent money at 5% interest per month, demanding the property of the Indians as security for the loan. The report noted that, whereas some of the Indians signed contracts voluntarily in order to supplement their income, others were forced to sign them to cancel debts. For example, the contractor would sell alcohol on credit, particularly on national holidays, obliging the debtor to sign the work contract. In other instances, debts were contracted on the actual estates. The landowner, in breach of the law, would maintain shops, bars, gaming centres and even brothels

42. Humberto Flores Alvarado, *Proletarizacion del Campesino de Guatemala*, Editorial Rumbos Nuevos, Guatemala, 1971, p.170.
43. Melville, op. cit., p.194.

84

within reach of the huts within the estates. The Indian might thus be tempted into further debts, and be compelled to undertake additional labour over and above his initial contract in order to cancel them. In addition, contractual obligations were often found to have been violated by the landowner in order to extort more labour from the Indian. For instance, if the labourer fell ill during his period on the estate, he would be forced to put in extra work days to make up for the lost time (even though the labour laws specify that it is the duty of the landowner to look after his work force, and pay wages on the days they are sick).

The contractors tended to make their approach several months before harvest time. They would arrive at the time of greatest concentration of Indians from the outlying villages in the municipal town centre on market day, and advance credit in either cash or food during the scarce months of June-August, in order to have a guaranteed work force between September and January. The contractor would give an advance payment (*anticipo*) of on average $10. At the same time he would give work cards to the Indians, registering the length of time for which the contract had been signed. The average contract was less than two months, though 15% of those contracted in this year had signed for up to four months.

On the estates, conditions were found to be far worse than required by law. While the law stipulated an eight-hour day, the average labourer together with his family would work for between 10-14 hours per day; though the law stipulated 48 hours paid leave per week, one day's rest would be given without pay. Workers were also cheated on the weights by which they were paid according to the amount of harvest produced (in Guatemala it is the custom to pay either a fixed daily wage or a fixed rate per job for a specific task: under the latter arrangement it is obviously easier to cheat the work force). From subsequent interviews in the village of San Ildefonso, Richard Appelbaum found that over half the peasants who claimed they had been cheated felt unable to protest, in fear of imprisonment or blacklisting that would prevent them receiving employment in future years. Appelbaum also received numerous complaints that conditions were insanitary, that the workers did not receive the rations provided for by law, that landowners did not pay return fares as they were legally obliged, and that compulsory deductions were illegally made from their wages in order to provide rudimentary medical treatment[44].

The laws referred to were from the 1947 Labour Code, several articles of which had been designed to protect the migrant worker. For instance, Art 33: the owner of the estate must pay for transport costs from the place of origin to the farm and back, and also provide food for the days worked on the estate. Arts 116 and 121: the work day must not exceed 8 hours, nor the week's work 48 hours, and all overtime must be remunerated with a 50% surcharge; with overtime, the work day must not exceed 12 hours. Art 90: total payment must always be made in legal currency, although in the case of peasant labourers up to 30% of payment could be made in kind. Art 139: women and children who

44. Appelbaum, Study on Seasonal Migration, Ministerio de Educacion, Guatemala, 1967.

accompany the head of family on estate labour must also be bound by a work contract. Reference was also made to the later Presidential Decree 570, that all contractors were forbidden to receive commissions and emoluments, and must be paid a fixed wage.

In 1970 the case of rural and particularly of migrant workers in Guatemala was taken up by the International Labour Organisation (ILO). This body presented to the Guatemalan government a report on 'Colonisation, Agrarian Transformation, Rural Development and Agricultural Labour', in which it emphasised the following severe shortcomings in systems of labour recruitment and working conditions:

a. Inappropriate recruitment systems.
b. Low wages out of proportion to the sacrifices that the migrant workers had to endure.
c. Sub-human conditions in the transport from place of origin to work place, and back.
d. Lodging and living conditions of the migrant workers and their families within the work places, which were totally unacceptable with regard to hygiene, health, education and morality.
e. Sicknesses easily contracted by the workers and their families, due to climactic differences and the almost complete absence of hygienic facilities.
f. The penury suffered by family members in their place of origin when they did not follow the family head, with all the consequences deriving from this situation.
g. The fact that it was impossible for children who accompanied the family head to continue the studies they had commenced in their place of origin.

The ILO urged that a new ruling be established concerning agricultural labour as a matter of urgency, and that minimum wages be established; that the Labour Inspectorates (*Inspectorias de Trabajo*) be reinforced, in order to ensure that minimum wages were paid, and agricultural contracts effectively controlled; that the phenomenon of rural migratory work be carefully studied; that transport conditions be improved significantly, with state subsidies if necessary; and that work inspectors should operate in all areas where there was a significant amount of migrant labour[45].

Since that time at least minimum wages have been established. They are wretchedly small. For cotton, sugar and cattle ranch workers, the minimum at the beginning of 1976 was $1.12 per day; for coffee workers it was even less, $1.04 per day. Little more than that has been done. An ILO-UN study has been commissioned but the results are not yet public. Labour Inspectorates are few and far between, and the attitude of the Ministry of Labour has proved intransigent towards labour conflict on the plantations (see Chapter III for the Ministry's ruling over the recent strike on the sugar plantations). An article in the

45. International Labour Office, *Informe al Gobierno de la Republica de Guatemala sobre Colonizacion, Transformacion Agraria, Desarrollo Rural y Trabajo Agricola*, Geneva, 1970.

Labour Code still declares illegal any strike by agricultural workers during harvest time, and it is of course only at harvest time that there is a significant work force on the plantations. The migrant worker thus has no security of tenure and no bargaining power.

To control the activities of the contractors, the 1947 Labour Code also stipulated that each one must have a legal permit, and must receive a fixed wage (Art 141). And the transporters must receive a licence from the Directorate of Transport.

In recent years the majority of contractors have held these permits, though some 33% do not. Studies in recent years have shown that the number of contractors is on the increase. The debt motive is still extremely strong. In the Huehuetenango area last year, whereas over half of the Indians went voluntarily to the contractors to offer their services, well over a third were still being contracted in the local market at strategic moments. The system of forcing the peasant into debt by advancing sums of between $5-15 is still very widely used. The money may be advanced as long as six months before the harvest. In such cases, the money was almost always paid by the landowner himself, advanced to the contractor who (in up to 90% of cases) still worked on a commission basis rather than a fixed wage. If the Indian failed to turn up to work, it was the contractor rather than the landowner who suffered, for the money would be deducted from his commission or wage.

Visits to estates themselves in 1976 showed that conditions could not have improved much since 1967. There were still complaints at cheating over weights, at failure to pay minimum wages (many cotton workers claimed they were only receiving US 80 cents per day), and over hygienic conditions (one group complained that so many children had died after a measles outbreak in the estate on which they were working that several people had already returned to their highland villages without completing contracts).

In his study on San Ildefonso Ixtahuacan, Richard Appelbaum noted in the mid 1960s that Indians would only undertake seasonal labour as a last resort. In 1976 a group of North American aid workers in Chimaltenango province also observed that, as soon as a peasant family could increase its production to subsistence level, it would forego the annual migration. Yet for almost all Indians in the northern provinces of Quiche, Huehuetenango and San Marcos, it has now become a part of life. Illegal methods of persuasion still have to be used — thus the growing number of contractors today — but the growing highland population, increased land parcelisation, and above all the appallingly inegalitarian land distribution and agrarian policies of the government have ensured that poverty and starvation provide a cheap labour force for the estates more successfully than did the legislation and brute force of the colonial and nineteenth-century periods.

The Cooperative Movement
Agricultural cooperatives first became widespread during the Arevalo government, and fell off after 1952. After 1954, the State attempted to control

cooperatives, which gained far greater importance after the virtual disappearance of the peasant leagues and rural unions. In 1957 an executive decree assigned to the Inspectorate of Banks (*Superintendencia de Bancos*) the responsibility of direction of and technical assistance to the cooperatives until a new law governing their organisation was passed. In 1959 the promotion and control of agricultural cooperatives was passed directly to the Ministry of Agriculture[46]. In the 1960s, however, a number of independent cooperatives were established among the Indian population in such provinces as Quiche and Chimaltenango. Progressive priests in particular saw the cooperative movement as a way of bringing the scattered population together to discuss problems other than agricultural techniques and food production, and to learn the values of communal living and communal decision-making in general. The movement came under frequent attack from right-wing political parties, and was accused of being a communist front (Amnesty International reported that "Vice-President Mario Sandoval Alarcon as well as former President Arana have repeatedly attacked the cooperatives as approaching communism")[47]. Some of the missionaries expelled from Guatemala in the late 1960s were charged specifically with the promotion of subversion through the cooperatives.

Over the last decade, the number of cooperatives has grown significantly. In July 1967, there were 145 actively functioning in the whole of the country, including the officially sponsored cooperatives in the Peten. By March 1976 there were 510 altogether, with a total membership of 132,116. Of these, 227 were agricultural cooperatives, 26 artisan, 192 savings and loan, and 86 consumer. 290 (or 57%) were in the Indian highland region, and 149 of the agricultural cooperatives (or 65.64% of this type) were likewise in the highlands (*altiplano*).

President Kjell Laugerud has given unprecedented support to the cooperative movement since his accession to power in 1974. He invited cooperative leaders to the presidential palace (an unaccustomed sight in Guatemala, where the peasant has rarely had such close access to the corridors of power) and he appointed as State Counsellor Jose Miguel Gaitan, a specialist in rural development working as a deputy manager of BANDESA, and an outspoken supporter of the cooperatives. In 1975 over US $6,000,000 were committed to the cooperatives, including a substantial $4,500,000 loan from AID for the purchase of fertiliser and other agricultural inputs. At the beginning of 1976, the Inter-American Development Bank signed an agreement with the Guatemalan government, for a loan of over $15,000,000 for cooperative development. According to a report from *INFORPRESS*, the programme was to be executed by BANDESA. It provided for direct credit to small and medium scale farmers, with "the provision of credit to cooperatives, cooperative federations, foundations and other legally constituted rural organisations, for the carrying out of small agro-industrial programmes, the installation of storage centres, and the realisation of agricultural programmes for affiliated members". Of the 27,000 small farmers expected to benefit, 5000 would be individuals, 22,000 cooperative members. A

46. Carole Snee, op. cit., p.44.
47. Amnesty International Briefing, *Guatemala*, December 1976.

further loan of $340,000 was agreed to strengthen the infrastructure of BANDESA[48]. And finally, the cooperative movement was given substantial aid after the February earthquake (for instance, the National Reconstruction Committee announced at the end of May 1976 that loans of $375,000 and $189,000 had been granted by the National Housing Bank (BANVI) to the cooperatives of Santa Lucia and 10 de Junio respectively).

There can be no doubt that sectors of the highland peasantry have been greatly strengthened both economically and politically by this unexpected degree of support. Credit and extension work have been a vital form of aid, and in Chimaltenango province the solidarity of the cooperatives against exploitation by the owners of the large wheat mills eventually persuaded the government to put up the price of wheat. Improved storage through the IDB programme could do much to cut out the speculation of the middleman, and to protect at least the cooperative members themselves against exorbitant prices for basic grains in the scarce months. Many cooperatives have established efficient marketing networks, and have also been able to decrease substantially the cost-price of fertiliser to their members, after bulk purchase.

Yet there is another less attractive side to the coin. As already observed the trade union movement has frequently expressed its strong opposition to the emphasis on cooperatives, not so much because they have been used as a political tool by the present administration (any politician anywhere would attempt to derive political advantage from popular measures), as because the ethic of the cooperative movement is built on advantage for the few at the expense of the many, and stands in the way of the desperately needed agrarian reform. The philosophy of the movement now rests on more intensive farming and the implantation of the business ethic, with advantage to the individual. Many critics have noted that the cooperative, when selling its grain on the open market, will always adopt a competitive attitude, and attempt to gain the highest possible price for the advantage of its own members. While the number of landless peasants increases, only those with some land and a degree of capital can join the cooperatives. Credit can only be obtained after initial capital deposit, and the credit given can only be a certain multiple of the initial deposit, thus creating a situation where private capital formation is essential, and where those with the greatest capital will also obtain the largest loans.

There is also justified criticism that the cooperatives have been used to increase cultural and political dependency. One North American analyst recently completed a study of a programme carried out in Guatemala by the Agricultural Cooperative Development International (ACDI), a private organisation acting under contract to AID. ACDI began its work in 1970, as part of Guatemala's rural development plan for the 1970s, taking as its target area the Indian highlands. Using Peace Corps volunteers among others, ACDI established the first of six regional cooperatives in the highlands, and by 1973 had extended this to five regional centres, which were organised in late 1973 into a regional

48. *INFORPRESS*, 29.1.1976.

agricultural cooperative federation, FECOAR. Within these organisations it was found that, although individual members had a vote, the fundamental policy decisions were all taken by a managing board which had been directly appointed by ACDI. The emphasis of educational programmes was on the maximisation of profits, the need for individual initiative, and the propagation of consumer goods such as radios, cigarettes and easy-remedy drugs which were held out as symbols of socio-economic advancement (a process known among Guatemalan sociologists as *ladinisation*, with emphasis on individual upward-mobility rather than the more traditionally Indian community consciousness). The writer then took a look at the composition of ACDI at its base in Washington. He found that, of 24 ACDI board members, 20 were members of large cooperative groups in the USA, five of which had been listed among the top 500 industrial corporations of that country. Not unnaturally, he concluded that the prime aim of the ACDI project was to bring the topmost sector of the Guatemalan peasantry within the echelons of international consumer society[49].

The major shortcomings of Guatemalan cooperativism should thus be clear. In a society where peasants are smallholders together, there are obvious benefits from the approach. In a society such as Guatemala's there are clear social benefits from cooperative work and farming, cooperative education and discussion — the basis of the early cooperativism that was so vigorously attacked by right-wing sectors. Though independent cooperatives are still to an extent following this approach, it is in some areas becoming increasingly difficult to distinguish the 'cooperatives' from the small agro-business favoured by farmers living above the subsistence level, who have nevertheless been denied access to credit and technical assistance in the past. It will be the property-owning peasantry rather than landless and sub-subsistence farmers who will benefit most from this new form of international aid, undoubtedly aimed at diverting attention from the pressing needs for agrarian reform.

Land Conflicts Today — The Multinationals Join In

In July 1976 the Conference of Guatemalan Bishops — who have normally tended to refrain from politically provocative statements — published a 58-page document, *Unidos en la Esperanza* ('United in Hope') containing perhaps the harshest ever church criticism of the intrinsic injustice and violence of the Guatemalan system. The section on land tenure at first made the now customary criticisms: that the vast majority of the land is in a few hands; that only a few timid efforts have been made to remedy this situation; that the oligarchy has persistently tried to maintain its privileged position at the cost of the marginalisation of the rest of the population; and that legislation currently in force is designed above all to protect private property. But the document then continued with a far more significant and disturbing statement:

But this situation, far from being resolved, is becoming more and more critical every day. A proof of this is the tensions that have arisen in the so-called

49. Taken from paper by Chris Rosene, *Look Who's Running the Coops*, 1976.

Development Zones (Izabal, El Peten, Alta Verapaz and Quiche) where continuous turmoil prevails. And this is because large landowners want to possess ever greater amounts and take over lands which have been acquired legitimately by those who have worked them for many years. *Perhaps the expectation of discovering oil in these regions has awakened immoderate ambitions and has sparked off an unjustified violence that we cannot refrain from denouncing.* Chisec, Moran, Nebaj and others are the names of places where peasants have died for the 'crime' of defending the land that they have possessed for a long time . . . [50]

Oil concessions were handed out to foreign companies up to twenty years ago, but it is only within the past couple of years that extensive explorations have been made, and the first large oil finds have occurred. At the same time, the new road from Huehuetenango to Izabal across the *Faja Transversal del Norte* has increased immeasurably the potential value of good but hitherto impenetrable agricultural land. This road is being constructed by three parties, the National Institute for Agrarian Transformation (INTA), the Army Engineering Corps, and finally (and most interestingly) the foreign-owned Shenandoah oil company[51]. Some commentators have claimed that this new road, over 200 kilometres in length, will be a "road of peasant liberation". The editor of *El Grafico*, however, has observed more realistically firstly that new landowners have secured property of up to 30 *caballerias* (334.5 acres) in the area quite recently, dislodging former peasant proprietors after presenting supplementary titles to the land; secondly that potential mineral wealth in the area is of more importance than the agricultural wealth; finally, that one of the major apparent purposes of the new road will be to provide a much-needed oil supply line for the huge new nickel mining complex at El Estor that is soon to be brought into operation by a consortium of multinational companies.

It is no surprise to find that the new road will pass through the area of Rubelsanto, where Shenandoah has made its first major oil find and is now commencing extraction. But significantly the areas of greatest rural violence over the past year have been precisely those affected by the road, and where oil exploration was also expected to take place. The English-language newspaper *Central America Report* stated in April 1976 that "the success at Rubelsanto has encouraged Shenandoah Petroleum Company to plan in the near future three more drillings in the adjacent areas of Chisec, Playa Grande and Xabal"[52].

On 6 January 1976, four peasants were assassinated in the village of Cakiha in the municipality of Chisec. According to the official version put out by government sources, members of the Border Patrol had been ambushed on a farm in the area, and had killed the peasants in the ensuing gun-fire. According to a statement signed by the Bishop of Verapaz and 43 other priests and nuns of the region, the official version was a deliberate distortion of the truth. Several armed men in

50. Mensaje del Episcopado Guatemalteco, *Unidos en la Esperanza*, Presencia de la Iglesia en la Reconstruccion de Guatemala, July 1976.
51. *INFORPRESS*, 5.8.1976.
52. *Central America Report*, 5.4.1976.

plain clothes, accompanied by peasants from a neighbouring cooperative, had either dragged the victims from their homes and later killed them, or assassinated them on the spot. According to the priests' version, the cause of the violence was one of the several land conflicts in the area, rising from the fact that peasant farmers had never been granted legal title to the land that they had worked for several years.

In the same month of January 1976 the first national publicity was given to mass disappearances that had taken place six months earlier in the community of Xalbal de Ixcan Grande, in the municipality of Chajul, Quiche province. The newspaper *La Nacion* published the first of two prepared articles (the second never appeared) on the disappearance of 37 members of the Xalbal agricultural cooperative (the article was based on statements by relatives of the missing people, who had been eye-witnesses to many of the events). Four peasants had been detained by uniformed paratroopers during the afternoon of 7 July 1975, and a further 33 had been detained during the course of that month. At the end of that year not one of them had reappeared, and the authorities denied that they had been arrested. A sworn statement signed by 25 members of the Xalbal cooperative had been delivered to President Laugerud on 12 November 1975 seeking his personal intervention, but to no effect.

At the end of April 1976 — after a period of escalating political violence throughout the country — members of the PR reported a campaign of military aggression and systematic intimidation of the peasantry in certain parts of Quiche, including the persecution of 300 PR affiliates. Christian Democrat leaders later backed up the charges, when their leader claimed in July 1976 that three CD leaders in the Quiche area had been kidnapped and later assassinated, during a repressive campaign launched against Quiche peasants accused of belonging to, or assisting, a guerrilla front. According to the CD leader, Luis Enrique Guillen Fuentes, the Guatemalan army were directly responsible for kidnappings and assassinations in the municipality of Cotzal, on June 25th. When a regional CD leader protested about these events, he too (said Guillen Fuentes) was kidnapped and assassinated by Guatemalan army detachments. These are just two of several recent allegations from the Quiche area. It appears that the brutality around the villages of Cotzal, Chajul and Nebaj commenced in February 1976, when one man was arrested carrying a revolver, a grenade and a compass. Assuming that this was a sign of guerrilla activity in the area, the army immediately commenced a military occupation of the region. According to evidence provided by a prominent US churchman to a US Congressional Hearing on Human Rights in Central America in June 1976:

On March 19th and 20th a group of armed men in civilian clothes, using two Toyota landrovers, passed unhindered through military roadblocks and kidnapped nine men from the villages of Cotzal, Chajul and Nebaj. On March 29th a mother of five children was abducted in a similar manner. All the victims have since disappeared. In addition, six deaths have been confirmed: three brothers aged 13, 18 and 22 were killed by a grenade in Nebaj and three other men were executed in their homes in Chichel on March 28th. In spite of the denunciations that have been made by members of the political opposition, church officials and others, no investigation appears to have been initiated . . .[53]

CNUS published a denunciation of the events that had been submitted to them by a number of peasants from the affected area. The report blamed the army and the Mobile Military Police for both torture and assassination:

On February 20th they captured Antonio Medina . . . he was tortured that same night in the Municipality of Chajul by members of the Mobile Military Police who came from Chajul, in the presence of municipal officials. On February 21st army helicopters scoured all the zone and soldiers from the military zone of Quiche entered and occupied Chajul and Cotzal . . . The terror has been increasing while the repression has been intensified through disappearances, tortures, abuses and deaths that have occurred in different parts of the region. It has reached a point where several families do not sleep at home, others have abandoned the cultivation of their land and others commerce, for fear of being detained . . .

The report continued with detailed descriptions of specific cases, the names of those arrested and missing. It also stated that, when relatives of the missing people went to the regional capital of Quiche to make representations to the authorities about the whereabouts of their relatives, they were met with blank faces, the authorities denying knowledge of the events[54].

At the national level the Ministers of Defence and the Interior at first denied knowledge of the alleged events at Ixcan, Chajul and Cotzal. When relatives of the missing people at Ixcan approached the Minister of Defence, Romeo Lucas, in January 1976, he admitted that an anti-subversive military operation had been carried out in Quiche in July 1975, and attributed the allegations to "the instigation of politicians who tend to denounce such fictitious events". In May 1976, the provincial governor of Quiche likewise denied that there had been any persecution of peasants. But in late August, after nationally publicised reports that a military detachment had been in a clash with members of the National Army, the government was forced to admit that military action had occurred in the Quiche province as part of counterguerrilla operations. In the latter cases then – and possibly also in the Ixcan case – the brutal intervention of the military was at least partially caused by their belief that peasants had been collaborating with guerrillas. In Ixcan, Amnesty International has noted that "there is no evidence of such cooperation, and no formal accusation of such activity by any of the residents at Xalbal was ever made"[55]. Whether or not such complicity existed, the above examples serve

53. Testimony of William L. Wipfler, of National Council of Churches of Christ in the USA, to Subcommittee on International Organisations of the Committee on International Relations of the House of Representatives, Hearings on Human Rights in Central America, June 1976.
54. Taken from *INFORPRESS*, 29.4.1976.
55. Amnesty International, Campaign for Abolition of Torture, 1976.

to show the extent of illegal force used against the indigenous peasantry by the authorities as well as private landowners, when the status quo is threatened. It may be more than a coincidence that these acts took place on disputed territory where value has been so greatly increased by new mineral exploitation and improved communications.

The more traditional agrarian conflict continues. The pattern tends to remain the same. Often the peasant group is able to produce a title to the land it claims, but the large farmer can produce an alternative title, plus lawyers and the threat of violence or the support of military and police authorities. Two typical cases are:

(a) Los Lirios Allotment, Masagua, Escuintla

(In this case peasants, who had occupied land here since 1954 and who were being threatened with eviction by a new landowner, reported their situation in a taped interview. The account given below is taken primarily from this tape-recording.)

In December 1953, over 4 *caballerias* (446 acres) were expropriated from Los Lirios farm, under Decree 900 of the Arbenz Agrarian Reform. The land was originally divided between 49 peasants, who received approximately 5 *manzanas* (8.6 acres) each in January 1954. After the Castillo Armas coup, a group of the peasants (now 30) were allowed to remain on a reduced portion of this land. An Agrarian Inspector decreed first of all that each peasant should be permitted to retain 2 *manzanas* (3.4 acres), though eventually all 30 peasants received only 32 *manzanas* between them. When the landowner appealed against the decision, the Appeal Court decreed that the land should be returned to him; but that compensation should be paid for the buildings constructed, for crops and improvements. He failed to do this, but rather left the peasants alone until 1962, when the farm was sold. The new owner took out a summary eviction order in 1964, but lost the case. The farm was again sold in 1970, to Santiago Pezzarossi (one of Guatemala's largest landowners, who is sole owner or share-holder of several properties in the Escuintla area). After attempting to evict the peasants, Pezzarossi took them to court on charges of being criminals and squatters, and demanded a substantial fine for damages to the land. The case was finally decided in favour of Pezzarossi in late 1975, by which time the peasants had been in possession of their own plots for over 21 years, and had won a court-case over ten years beforehand.

But this time the fight was taken up by sympathisers in Escuintla, and by the trade union and student movement throughout the country. A much-publicised letter to the President of the Republic tied the Los Lirios case up with rural violence in the remainder of the country, expressing the fear that the "Chisec case will be repeated in the allotment of Los Lirios where there were not five potential victims but many more". The letter demanded that: (i) those found guilty of the Chisec assassinations should be punished in accordance with the law; (ii) that peasants both in Chisec and in Los Lirios should not be dispossessed of their lands, but that their respective property rights should be duly authorised;

and (iii) that the systematic eviction of peasants should cease.

(b) Comuneros of Jalapa

A second case occurred in Jalapa (a more predominantly *mestizo* area) towards the end of 1975. Violence again flared up in Santa Maria Xalapan, the area where several peasants had died in a clash with the army in the village of Sansirisay in 1973, after cultivators of communal land (*comuneros*) had claimed that their own territory was being usurped by recently arrived cattle farmers. The earlier conflict had been sparked off when the cattle ranchers deliberately let their cattle loose among the maize fields of the *comuneros*, who (according to press reports) appropriated them and took them to the municipal headquarters, to prove that their lands had been invaded. The military commander of the region had then ordered a detachment of the Mobile Military Police to investigate the problems. When violence subsequently broke out, it was estimated that 6 policemen and a minimum of 25 peasants were killed[56]. It will be remembered that the Arana government had provided a temporary solution to the problems by purchasing some of the land and distributing it to the *comuneros* of the region.

Conflict over the ownership of this land had existed since the early 18th century. The *comuneros* claimed that they had been given title to 400 *caballerias* of land in the colonial period, and they were also able to show a title from 1911, this time conceding them ownership of over 18 *caballerias* of land. Yet it appears that at the beginning of this century, when the provincial boundaries were altered, new owners began to lay claim to those parts of the communal land that were now located within the new province of El Progreso.

On 19 September 1975 the *comuneros* began to invade the neighbouring lands to which they laid claim, arguing that their numbers — now exceeding 40,000 — produced a desperate need to recover land which had been illegally appropriated. Their legal adviser, Jesus Marroquin, declared shortly afterwards to the press that both he and the community leader had received anonymous murder threats. As Marroquin's predecessor, Gregorio Fuentes Charnaud, had been assassinated at the time of the 1973 conflict, he had every reason to take the threats seriously. At the time of writing the outcome is not known.

4. Conclusions

There can be no swift remedy for Guatemala's agrarian problem. For its foreign exchange earnings, the country relies on the export of commercial cash crops, which are monopolised by a few wealthy landowners, most of whom have extensive business and financial interests outside the agricultural sector. The agro-export sector relies on a cheap agricultural labour force, and remains bitterly opposed to any structural reforms which might threaten its privileged position. With poverty and malnutrition having reached such disastrous levels, the initial results of agrarian transformation would be greater local consumption, and an inevitable drop in foreign exchange earnings.

56. Taken from reports in *La Tarde* and *El Grafico*, 25-29 May, 1973.

The present situation, with its roots in the colonial days but more particularly in the late nineteenth-century liberal period, shows the disaster engendered by concentrating on increased agricultural production *per se*, if there is neither agrarian reform, nor alternative employment off the land, nor a legal or political mechanism by which the interests of agricultural workers can be represented. In 1977 (although forced labour legislation has been replaced by the compulsions of capitalist-induced poverty) the injustice in rural areas is surely as great as that which prevailed during the Ubico dictatorship of the 1930s and 1940s. By all accounts the land tenure disparities are greater than they were thirty years ago.

Although legislation has been passed nationally to provide for improved labour conditions, and while some international conventions of the ILO have been ratified by the Guatemalan government, there has been no attempt to ensure that such legislation is enforced. Instead, violence has been used widely to preserve the status quo, and prevent the resurgence of otherwise unavoidable serious rural upheaval.

The cooperative movement has brought some improvements, though not to the poorest groups of farmers. Agrarian tensions will not subside until land is made available to the landless, and until independent rural organisations are permitted to play an active part in the country's political life instead of being regarded as a subversive threat. The outlook is certainly pessimistic. But rural organisations, though severely repressed since 1954, have never been entirely eliminated. The Peasant Leagues (*Ligas Campesinas*) survive; a number of indigenous movements are growing in strength; and peasant organisations are playing an increasingly important role in CNUS. One effect of this is that their demands are being voiced more frequently in the national media. The example from Jalapa (page 94) depicts the predicament facing lawyers who attempt to intervene on behalf of the peasantry. Threats are widespread, and both intimidation and the incapacity of the peasantry to pay for legal aid have usually guaranteed that the landowner wins cases brought before the courts. The intimidation of rural organisations has been a further decisive factor in the landlord's interest. A group of young lawyers have now formed a legal aid organisation designed specifically to help peasants who could not otherwise afford the costs of legal aid, but if they take on politically sensitive cases there can be no certainty that they will escape the violence with which CNUS legal advisers have recently been confronted.

At the time of writing, three news cuttings which reflect the continuing crisis facing Guatemala's rural population were received from Guatemala. In the first (of May 1977) local officials from Alta Verapaz province had protested to the Minister of Agriculture at the ruthless manner in which other officials acting in the name of the Agrarian Transformation Institute (INTA) had evicted peasants from land which they had traditionally occupied, and granted it to "influential individuals" with government connections. In the second (also of May 1977) representatives of a number of rural unions from the coastal sugar estates had presented a petition to Congress, urging the dismissal of three labour judges who had consistently made "biased" judgments in the landowners' favour. In the third (of July 1977) 500 peasant families had invaded part of a large coastal estate, claiming that it was public land bordering the coast, which had been cordoned off illegally by the estate owner. The peasants had invaded the same land before, but had on that occasion been driven off by the police.

V Relating Foreign Aid to Human Rights:
The Relevance of Guatemala

1. Introduction

This report has been concerned with problems of violations of human rights in the broadest possible sense. Though much space has been devoted to listing specific atrocities in recent years, it has been equally concerned with deep rooted and institutionalised structural problems. For the majority of Guatemalans, as for other Latin American peoples, human rights are seen not only as the right to life, to protection from such abuses as torture and arbitrary arrest; but also as the rights to freedom of organisation, to land, employment, health and education.

Over the past few years there has been much international debate on the role played by foreign governments and organisations in supporting repressive regimes in Latin America and possible ways in which foreign governments (primarily the United States) might consider applying human rights criteria to their foreign aid policies. The debate has been conducted at various levels. Governments which have traditionally used military and economic aid as a means to further their own strategic interests abroad, eschewing considerations of human rights, are under pressure from humanitarian lobbies within their own countries to modify their aid policies. At the other end of the scale even small private and non-governmental organisations, which often form those same lobbies, have sometimes been criticised themselves for continuing their aid and development projects within repressive societies. As Latin American society has become increasingly polarised, and military or military-backed regimes exercise more control over all aspects of their country's economic life, all aid — however neutral it may appear at first sight — assumes a political dimension.

While most people would now accept that the international community has a right and a duty to speak out against gross violations of civil and political rights (as in the cases of Chile or Uganda), far fewer believe that violations of social and economic rights should be treated in the same way. Although there is increasing international recognition of third world demands for a new international economic order, there is less concern that economic and social justice *within* a third world country should be regarded as an internationally recognised human right. The implication is that, whereas a government may be held responsible for specific atrocities, social and economic conditions are a consequence of historical developments and are not caused directly by the policies of any one government. And in theory, if civil and political freedoms were guaranteed, then the most deprived members of an inegalitarian society would be able to organise within a western-style democratic structure and fight for their basic rights.

But in practice, police states often emerge precisely when vested economic interests are threatened, particularly when (as in Guatemala in the early 1950s) strong worker organisations have been established under sympathetic left-leaning governments and have threatened a radical transformation of society. When this leads to military intervention (as in Guatemala since 1954) an escalation of violence and repression would seem inevitable as worker organisations attempt to regroup and make demands unacceptable to powerful economic interest groups. In such cases international campaigns for the protection of human rights, if they are to have any effect whatsoever, cannot simply be an expression of humanitarian concern but must assume a political dimension, becoming a form of intervention in so far as the oppressed groups are actively supported. This view was expressed by the World Council of Churches at its 1975 Fifth Assembly:

> In our work for human rights we often tend to tackle the symptoms rather than the basic causes. While we must endeavour to put an end to particular violations of human rights, such as torture, we must bear in mind that inequitable social structures —as manifested in, for example, economic exploitation, political manipulation, the exercise of military power, domination by one class — create the conditions under which human rights are violated. Work for human rights must therefore entail the foundation of a society free of unjust structures.

Anyone who subscribes to such views would obviously question the effectiveness of diplomatic pressure as a means to improve the human rights situation in any one country. Diplomatic approaches rest on the premise that a repressive government can somehow be persuaded to restore a rule of law, under which organised pressure groups, such as the trade unions, will within a democratic structure be enabled to reorganise and press for much-needed social and economic reforms. Yet up to now foreign governments and organisations have never been able to exercise effective pressure to guarantee the protection of even civil and political rights in another country. At the present moment the machinery of the inter-governmental organisations for the protection of human rights (such as the United Nations Human Rights Commission or the Human Rights Commission of the Organisation of American States) has been rendered virtually ineffective by tactical alliances between member countries. To date the one initiative which has apparently had serious repercussions within Latin America has been the unilateral 'human rights offensive' of the Carter administration in the United States, following US Congressional resolutions that both military and economic aid should be tied to human rights guarantees. It is far too early to judge the effectiveness of the limited measures so far taken but, in the few cases where military aid has been restricted on human rights grounds, the affected Latin American governments have rejected any US demands as an intolerable intervention in their internal affairs, and claimed that other sources of military credits and sales are readily available to them. At the same time there are numerous indications that the US Government is not willing to take steps that would seriously mar its relations with friendly Latin American governments.

The US initiative has so far focused principally on the limitation or denial of aid to governments that violate human rights. The proponents of these new policies have argued largely from the standpoint of enlightened self-interest, claiming that the long-term interests of the American people have not been served by support for repressive dictatorships which, in Latin America as in South East Asia, are certain to be ephemeral. Sceptics on the right have argued that strategic interests cannot be sacrificed overnight on unrealistic humanitarian grounds; sceptics on the left have argued that strategic interests *will* not be sacrificed since, in the final analysis, issues of hemispheric security and economic advantage will always override humanitarian considerations.

The US administration has, however, also been keen to show that human rights factors are taken into account in its economic aid policies as a whole. The United States Agency for International Development (AID) has been advised to look for individual development projects which contain a human rights component. Whenever an application for funds is received, one of the suggested criteria for its assessment should be the effect that the project would have on the overall human rights situation in the particular country.

A similar line has been taken by the development agencies of some other countries which have less economic investment within Latin America, and are correspondingly less able to influence government policy there, but which nevertheless have ongoing aid programmes. The Netherlands Minister for Development Cooperation, J.P. Pronk, has admitted the essentially interventionist character of all development aid and has likewise argued that human rights must be an important criterion in the selection of projects. But unlike the US government, which seeks reasons for continuing its aid to repressive governments, the Dutch Minister placed the emphasis on giving aid to non-governmental sources in countries where human rights were violated. He also stressed that the US Congressional human rights initiative was based on a limited concept of human rights and that insufficient attention was paid to social justice. To quote some excerpts from an article recently published by the Dutch Minister in an international human rights journal:

In Latin America and elsewhere we see in a dramatic way how people set about achieving social justice, how they need to exercise political freedoms to do this, and how they are oppressed and become the victims of inhuman tortures... Development aid means working for fairer social structures — a matter of fundamental importance as regards human rights; it also means giving direct aid to the victims of violation of human rights, among them political prisoners and refugees. The basic approach — common endeavours to achieve fairer social structures — is sought in Dutch development aid in the emphasis that is placed on the human rights criterion for the selection of target countries and in the support given to groups and organisations actively promoting equal rights and justice in political and socio-economic matters ... Human rights must be understood in their totality, and in the relation between political freedom and social justice. I consider it only right that development aid should be linked with human rights in this broader sense. Thinking in some circles of the US Congress is proceeding on similar lines, particularly in the Subcommittee on International Organisations and Movements of the House of Representatives Foreign Affairs Committee. Among the methods recommended by the Subcommittee for bringing pressure to bear on governments guilty of gross violations of human rights was the threat to end certain economic aid programmes. I feel I should add the view that this recommendation, however important, seems to be based on a limited view, being concerned only with violations of civil and political rights. In my view attention must also be paid to the requirement of social justice. It will be clear that I do not believe that development aid can be neutral in character. Development aid must set in motion processes through which the poor and oppressed can achieve freedom and the right to a say in their own affairs . . . The New International Economic Order cannot fully achieve its goal unless the necessary structural changes in international economic relations are accompanied by radical social reform[1].

The British Overseas Development Ministry (ODM), whose aid programmes have customarily been concentrated in former British colonies, has never had more than a modest programme in Latin America. Its overall strategy for bilateral aid has been to focus on the poorest countries, defined in terms of per capita income, which would exclude all Latin American countries with the exception of Haiti and Bolivia. Since 1970 it has however expanded its Latin America aid programme and by 1976 was expending £20,000,000 in bilateral aid. Though human rights terminology *per se* has not been used by the ODM in the formulation of its foreign aid policies, a new policy paper of October 1975 stressed that more attention should be paid to small-scale rural development projects and to structural problems within rural areas:

There is an important difference between concentrating on increased agricultural production *per se* and increased agricultural production through the medium of rural development. The latter should involve an improvement of the standard of life of the broad mass of the rural population . . . Within the rural sector, therefore, one might expect greater emphasis on projects designed to benefit the rural poor such as the poor small farmers and the landless labourers[2].

At present however only a small proportion of British aid is channelled to the "poorest sectors". In many areas, particularly former British colonies and territories in associated status, substantial British aid funds are still used for security needs, in the provision of such items as police equipment and training. Human rights factors are rarely considered in the allocation of aid, and decisions in this respect are still taken largely on an ad hoc basis. Though pressure was brought to bear on the British government to deny further military equipment to the Chilean junta after the military coup of September 1973, this has been a somewhat isolated instance and the result of concerted pressure from politically powerful sectors in Britain including the trade union movement (and even then there was some debate within the trade union movement itself, as to whether humanitarian concerns could override the issue of national economic interest).

1. From International Commission of Jurists Review, June 1977, *Human Rights and Development Aid* by J.P. Pronk.
2. Ministry of Overseas Development, *The Changing Emphasis in British Aid Policies: More Help for the Poorest,* October 1975.

A similar instance occurred in mid 1977 when the British National Union of Miners (NUM) was largely instrumental in persuading the British government to cancel a projected £19,000,000 grant to the Bolivian State Mining Corporation COMIBOL. An NUM delegation had made an unofficial visit to Bolivia shortly beforehand, at a time when the Bolivian Miners' Federation had been taken over by the military government and many of its leaders imprisoned or exiled. The NUM argued that the provision of such a grant, if not strongly tied to human rights guarantees, would serve only to reinforce the position of the Bolivian government and weaken that of the miners' union. However, had the NUM not visited Bolivia at precisely the time when the ODM was planning its biggest ever single loan to a Latin American country it is doubtful whether there would have been any appreciable public or parliamentary debate on the human rights implications of such a project.

While aid-donor governments are coming under greater pressure to apply human rights considerations to their foreign aid programmes, there are also indications that in Europe no less than the USA (see below) bilateral aid is becoming statistically far less significant than multilateral aid through the international financial institutions. In July 1976 the UK (together with West Germany, Spain, Belgium, Denmark, Israel, Switzerland, Yugoslavia and Japan) attained full non-regional membership of the Inter-American Development Bank (IDB), which together with the World Bank is by far the largest source of international credits to Latin American governments. Austria, Holland, Italy and France attained the same non-regional membership at a later date. Britain was to take up US $61,600,000 of share capital in the IDB and was also to contirbute US $61,600,000 to the Fund for Special Operations, the soft loan fund of the IDB (both these contributions were to be made from the normal overseas aid budget). In a press release issued on the day of Britain's joining the IDB, the ODM emphasised the commercial advantage to be derived from membership:

In joining the Bank, Britain will not only ensure an effective and productive channel for certain of her future aid funds to Latin America and the Caribbean, but will also open up a large new procurement market for her exporters since, as a result of membership, all IDB-financed contracts (with the exception of a small amount of tied money already pledged) will now become open to British contractors, consultants and suppliers.

This is a reminder that any nation's overseas aid policies will tend to be based fundamentally on motives of self-interest, and some return will normally be expected from the money invested. Though this will include returns of political advantage, only major world powers can afford to see aid in this light. The less wealthy the aid-donor nation, the more likely it is to use aid to further its commercial interests both at home and abroad. Rural development projects, offering less attractive sales prospects, are a poor competitor. And even in rural development, it seems likely that there will be a continued concentration on technical assistance involving the provision of specialised equipment, fertiliser etc., which can be administered far more easily and efficiently to large agro-industrial schemes than to individual small farmers and cooperatives. The loans and grants of most aid-donor countries are tied to goods and services produced in their own countries to foster exports. Small-scale projects will inevitably provide less opportunities for tied credits or high-level technical assistance which aid-donor governments have traditionally wished to provide.

It is also difficult to assess the effectiveness of small-scale projects, where the problems are essentially structural. The major obstacles to progress are not so much the absence of skills and equipment as the lack of land, credit and market-ing facilities, and the denial of the right to the organisation which is so essential if the rural population is to play a larger part in decision-making. For these reasons small-scale rural development projects have tended to be the province of private aid agencies (which concern themselves more with programmes of literacy and critical education programmes, as the groundwork to rural organisation) than of official agencies (which normally need government approval for their aid programmes). In this sense, aid and human rights issues become inextricably intertwined and the foreign agencies involved may find themselves treading on politically sensitive ground. One development worker in Latin America described the problems succinctly in the following words:

Both the broadening of the scope and efficiency in the exercise of repression is bringing within its orbit types of development action which are not normally associated with human rights by most people. Such activities as programmes of rural health, agricultural improvement, technical formation, community organi-sation and human promotion in general are being subject to political inter-vention and harassment on an increasing scale. This particularly applies to those programmes which organise groups at a primary and secondary level with a view to giving an effective voice to the demands of the urban and rural poor. The only response available to many of the groups promoting such activities, particularly where repression is severe, is adaptation of their programme to less abrasive goals, or subversion.

Though foreign governments have concerned themselves little with these issues in the allocation of aid, there is in theory a network of international machinery to protect the organisational rights of rural workers. On paper, a number of Conventions of the International Labour Organisation are concerned specifically with the rights of association and the rights to adequate remuneration in rural areas. In recent years, some attempts have been made to strengthen the language of these Conventions. As long ago as 1969, for example, the Special Committee on Agrarian Reform of the Food and Agriculture Organisation (FAO) requested the International Labour Organisation (ILO) to

pay specific attention to removing restrictions on freedom of association of rural workers, identifying problems of structure and association for such workers, strengthening rural organisations through various educational activities and promoting closer association between trade unions and cooperatives as well as between urban trade unions and rural organisations[3].

Several years later, in 1975, the International Labour Conference of the ILO adopted a 'Convention concerning Rural Workers and their Role in Economic and Social Development' (Convention 141). Whereas previous ILO Conventions had referred only to the equal rights of association for rural workers as for any other group of workers, Convention 141 of 1975 states more explicitly that:

It shall be an objective of national policy concerning rural development to facilitate the establishment and growth, on a voluntary basis, of strong and independent organisations of rural workers, without discrimination as defined in the Discrimination Convention, 1958, in economic and social development and in the benefits resulting therefrom.

The International Labour Office presented a lengthy preliminary report to the 1974 International Labour Conference, in which it assessed the major obstacles to the development of rural organisations. In Latin America, for example, in only a few countries did the labour laws expressly recognise that all rural workers and persons engaged in agriculture had the right to form unions. In almost all cases, there was inadequate machinery for the implementation of labour laws in rural areas, or provision for sanctions against landowners and employers who prevented peasant organisations from carrying out their legitimate functions.

There is little that the ILO can do alone to implement these principles. At the time of writing Convention 141 had not (as far as is known) been ratified by any Latin American government. It does however provide a useful framework for governments which now claim to apply human rights criteria in foreign policy. Human rights cannot be interpreted narrowly and must go far beyond the basic rights of freedom from arbitrary arrest and torture, and the other civil and political rights which have up till now been at the forefront of international human rights discussions. This introduction has given a brief outline of the problems involved. We continue with a more detailed analysis of US human rights initiatives since 1973 and their relevance to a country like Guatemala. We shall then look at other human rights and aid initiatives within the Guatemalan context, including the role of non-governmental organisations as well as official human rights and development agencies.

2. The US Initiative
Between the 1950s and 1970s the US administration has granted thousands of millions of dollars in military aid to Latin American governments, primarily for counter-insurgency purposes. During the 1960s in particular the essential yardstick for such aid was internal and hemispheric security against the proliferating leftist guerrilla groups, and US military advisers became increasingly directly involved in counter-insurgency campaigns. Moreover, large numbers of Latin American military and police officers were trained in intelligence operations and

3. Cited in ILO preliminary report to 1974 ILO Conference, *Organisations of Rural Workers and their Role in Economic and Social Development.*

counter-insurgency at the International Police Academy in Washington, at military bases within the USA and at the US Army School of the Americas and Fort Gulick in Panama. Within individual Latin American countries, military aid and training programmes were under the control of the US Military Assistance Advisory Groups (MAAG) or military missions in each country, which had over-all country responsibility for the Military Assistance Programme (MAP). One estimate gives a total of 64,000 Latin Americans trained under the MAP in the USA and Panama between 1950-73, while thousands more received US-sponsored training within their own countries[4]. A substantial part of the training curriculum was devoted to interrogation techniques at a time when the use of torture was escalating throughout Latin America. Whether or not the US training involved specific instruction in torture techniques, there can be no disputing the fact that it was designed to increase the operational efficiency of countries known to practise torture.

In recent years, due largely to pressure from US Congressional human rights lobbies, donations through MAP have been reduced. In Guatemala, for example, MAP figures were down from US $1,177,000 in 1970 and $1,864,000 in 1971 to a projected $200,000 in 1976. On the other hand Foreign Military Sales (FMS) credits have continued to be substantial and in some Latin American countries are on the increase. In the words of one author:

> While MAP has declined, military exports under the FMS Programme have boomed to a high of $12 billion in fiscal 1975. Sales to Latin America have been increasing at a spectacular rate: from an average of $30 million yearly in the 1960s, to $72 million in fiscal 1971, $118 million in fiscal 1974 and a projected $180 million in fiscal 1976[5].

During the Nixon and Ford administrations, there was a constant battle between some sectors of Congress and the Executive on the question of military aid. While many individual congressmen tried to introduce amendments either reducing military aid or tying it to certain guarantees, the executive branch either through presidential veto or by finding loopholes in existing legislation sought to continue its policies. Though some concessions were made to the demands of public opinion, the US President and the State Department were reluctant to abandon their fundamental criterion — that security issues and the strategic importance of maintaining good relations with friendly military regimes in Latin America should override all human rights considerations. But despite the intransigence of Secretary of State Kissinger during the Nixon and Ford admini-strations, strong pressure from the legislative branch of government (itself influenced by domestic public opinion in the aftermath of Watergate and the Vietnam war) had considerable impact on foreign policy even before Carter's accession to the presidency. It is worth describing the background to this in some detail.

4. NACLA Report, January 1976, *The Pentagon's Protegees: US Training Programmes for Foreign Military Personnel,* p.10.
5. Ibid, p.9.

In March 1974 the Congressional Committee on Foreign Affairs published a report, 'Human Rights in the World Community: a Call for US Leadership'. The report claimed that the prevailing attitude towards foreign policy had led "the United States into embracing governments which practise torture and unabashedly violate almost every human rights guarantee pronounced by the world community" and argued that right-wing regimes were not durable and that the US government was damaging both its own prestige and its own long-term interests by supporting them. The report contained a number of substantive recommendations. First it was argued that the State Department should treat human rights factors as a regular part of foreign policy decision-making, and should set up an administrative structure to facilitate objective monitoring of the human rights situation throughout the world. An office for human rights should be created within the Department's Bureau of International Affairs, and a human rights officer assigned to each regional bureau of the Department (these officers should be responsible not only for monitoring the situation, but also for making foreign policy recommendations). Furthermore the State Department should set up its own Advisory Committee on Human Rights with representatives from non-governmental organisations and the academic world to advise on US policy. To put direct pressure on foreign governments guilty of gross violations of human rights, the State Department should take measures ranging from private consultation with and public intervention in United Nations agencies, to withdrawal of military assistance and sales and withdrawal of certain economic assistance programmes. Normal diplomatic relations with the governments concerned should be maintained. The State Department should also take positive steps to reinforce the international machinery for the protection of human rights by strengthening both the United Nations Human Rights Commission, and the Inter-American Human Rights Commission of the Organisation of American States. In addition the State Department should give financial support to international non-governmental organisations, provided that (among other things) it did not make its funding decisions according to political considerations and did not seek to undermine the objectives of these organisations.

From 1973 onwards the US Congressional Foreign Affairs Subcommittee on International Organisations has held its own hearings on the human rights situation in individual countries. By 1977 hearings had been held on Argentina, Brazil, Chile, Paraguay, Uruguay and the three Central American countries already mentioned (in Latin America alone). Congressmen have heard ample testimony concerning torture, political imprisonment and other abuses, and have also been able to discuss in open forum the role played by official US aid programmes in supporting repressive governments. Largely as a result of these hearings, the Foreign Assistance Acts since 1973 contained a clause (Section 32) that it was the "sense of Congress" that the US President should deny any economic or military assistance to the government of a foreign country that "practises the internment or imprisonment of that country's citizens for political purposes". Section 502B of the 1974 Foreign Assistance Act recommended that military assistance be denied to countries committing gross violations of human rights unless there were "extraordinary" reasons requiring such assistance (among examples of gross violations of human rights were torture, cruel or degrading treatment, and prolonged detention without charge). If assistance were to be given despite the evidence of gross violations of human rights, then the President must explain to Congress the exact nature of the circumstances that warranted the continuation of military aid. In 1975 Congress enacted further legislation, the International Food and Assistance Act, now included as Section 116 of the Amended Foreign Assistance Act, by which economic aid was denied to countries committing gross violations of human rights unless there were adequate reasons for believing that the aid is "directly beneficial to needy people"[6].

The so-called Carter initiative, which has received so much international publicity in recent months, is not the moralistic or opportunistic impulse of one man but has a number of antecedents. Before Carter's access to the presidency the US Department of State responded to Congressional demands by setting up a human rights administrative structure both in Washington and in US missions abroad, and also commissioned a report on the human rights situation in 82 countries that received US military aid during the previous year (a report eventually published under the Carter administration in March 1977). But whereas the Nixon and Ford administrations had been antagonistic to human rights pressures from Congress, the Carter administration has given its full support and taken the human rights issue even further than many Congressmen would have desired. And it is interesting to note that, while previously the US administration had concentrated exclusively on civil and political rights, both President Carter and Secretary of State Cyrus Vance have been willing at least to mention social and economic rights in their speeches before international organisations and public forums, and have indicated that repressive governments may be held responsible for social and economic injustice. The point was made by Cyrus Vance, for instance, in a speech in April 1977:

Let me define what we mean by 'Human Rights'. First there is the right to be free from governmental violation of the integrity of the person. Such violations include torture, cruel, inhuman or degrading treatment or punishment, and arbitrary arrest or imprisonment. And they include denial of fair public trial, and invasion of the home. Second, there is the right to the fulfilment of such vital needs as food, shelter, health care and education. We recognise that the fulfilment of this right will depend, in part, upon the stage of a nation's economic development. But we also know that this right can be violated by a government's action or inaction – for example, through corrupt official processes which divert resources to an elite at the expense of the needy, or through

6. For two detailed accounts of US Congress Human Rights measures in recent years, see: *Human Rights Legislation and United States Foreign Policy*, by David Weissbrodt, in Georgia Journal of International and Comparative Law, Vol. 7, 1977; and *The Parliamentary Role in Implementing International Human Rights: a US Example*, by John Salzburg and Donald D. Young, in Texas International Law Journal, Vol. 12, Nos. 2 and 3, 1977.

indifference to the plight of the poor. Third there is the right to enjoy civil and political liberties — freedom of thought; of religion; of assembly; freedom of speech; freedom of the press; freedom of movement both within and outside one's country; freedom to take part in government. Our policy is to promote all these rights . . .[7]

Cyrus Vance also emphasised that the United States "looks to use of economic assistance —whether bilateral or through international financial institutions — as a means to foster basic human rights", and stated that the Carter administration had proposed a 20% increase in US foreign economic assistance for fiscal year 1978.

But as we have already seen, the major concern of human rights lobbyists was not so much that there should be more aid, as that it should be diverted to the more needy sectors and should be subject to Congressional vetting to ensure that it should not reach repressive governments. At the beginning of 1977 a private Washington-based group, the Centre for International Policy, published a detailed and highly critical report, 'Foreign Aid: Evading the Control of Congress'. It asserted that, despite the legislation of the past few years, some 69% of US and multilateral foreign aid now reaching the third world did so without any prior Congressional review of planned country-by-country allocations:

In fiscal year 1976 the Third World got $24.9 billion in direct credits, government-guaranteed loans, government-insured investments and official debt deferments from 15 separate US bilateral programmes and US-supported multi-lateral agencies, of which Congress debated, authorised and appropriated country allocations for $7.7 billion, only 31.7% of the total. The remaining $17.2 billion or 69% was allocated by 11 semi-autonomous, self-sustaining US government corporations or international banks ranging from the Export-Import Bank of the United States to the World Bank and the International Monetary Fund. All are public agencies. All make obligations fully guaranteed by the public. Yet with few exceptions the selection of aid recipients by these agencies has gone unchecked by the US Congress or any other national legislature, while their spending has doubled in the last six years[8].

The total figure of $24.9 billion represented only official credits provided or contributed to by the US government, and omitted all private US loans and investment.

The report observed that, because of these loopholes, the Chilean government received no less than $357,000,000 in credits, guarantees and insurance, of which the US Congress had only authorised 21%, over the previous fiscal year (in other circles much publicity was given to Congressional resolutions withdrawing all

7. From speech by Cyrus Vance at University of Georgia, 30 April 1977, *Human Rights and Foreign Policy*, reproduced by the European Parliament in May 1977 for use by the Joint Working Group on Human Rights.
8. *Foreign Aid: Evading the Control of Congress*, from International Policy Report, Centre for International Policy, Washington DC, Vol. 3, No. 1.

further military aid to the Chilean government, and placing a ceiling of $25,000,000 on economic aid). It observed that only six of the sixteen major foreign aid channels were covered by the existing legislation tying aid to human rights guarantees, and that over the past six years the share of traditional aid outlets had dropped from 46% to 31% while more and more foreign aid had been channelled through the large US and international financial institutions such as the Export-Import Bank, the World Bank (International Bank for Reconstruction and Development) and the International Monetary Fund. Congress was thus able to review only a small part of the total programme, "as a result, Congress is all but shut out of effective decision-making on foreign economic policy".

Congress has taken steps to tackle this problem. In 1976 Congressman Tom Harkin pushed through the 'Harkin Amendment' requiring US delegates to the Inter-American Development Bank to vote against loans to governments guilty of a "consistent pattern of gross violations of internationally recognised human rights", making exceptions only for aid that was "directed specifically for programmes which serve the basic human needs of citizens" in countries where human rights were violated (presumably to the elimination of balance of payments credits, and much of the infrastructural credits that tend to dominate the loans of the international financial institutions). In 1977 the content of the Harkin Amendment was extended to other international institutions including the World Bank (reportedly against the wishes of President Carter himself, who now felt that the Congressional human rights campaign was going too far).

These developments are potentially the most important of all. In recent years, the amount of US bilateral military and economic aid to almost all Latin American countries has decreased. Direct military aid is being phased out, while economic aid is being directed increasingly to small-scale development projects (see below). At the same time, in the words of the Centre for International Policy, "nearly one-third of the $9 billion the World Bank expects to lend in fiscal 1979 will go to what it considers the 15 most repressive regimes. The accusation is based on the Bank's own documents"[9].

What relevance can the US human rights initiative have for other aid-donor countries? Most critics argue that, in Latin America particularly, the US must be considered separately because of its economic and political influence in the hemisphere, and because of its responsibility for establishing repressive regimes in the past. The attitude is symbolised in a recent editorial in *The Times*, entitled 'Human Rights in Latin America':

President Carter is uneasily conscious that most of the Latin American military regimes came into power with a degree of United States encouragement and support. In raising the issue of human rights, therefore, he is not gratuitously intervening in the internal affairs of the countries in question but trying to undo some of the damage done by earlier interference. Already he has cut military aid to some of the worst offenders (and they have reacted by voluntarily renouncing US military aid altogether). The next step, logically, is to make economic aid

9. Ibid.

conditional on specific improvements in respect for human rights. In Britain we can no longer exercise significant leverage over Latin America as a whole. A possible exception is Bolivia[10].

(The editorial goes on to recommend that the projected £19,000,000 grant to the Bolivian State Mining Corporation should be made conditional on the release of arrested miners, the return of political exiles, and guarantees of freedom of association in the future.)

The Times may be correct to say that the British government can alone exercise little leverage, but we should not overlook the importance of the British and other European votes in the multilateral financial institutions. We have already seen that in Latin America, the UK no less than the USA is now allocating a substantial amount of its aid funds through such organisations as the World Bank and the Inter-American Development Bank. The UK is one of the largest contributors to the World Bank and is thus in a position to influence its policy. Though the UK has less than 1% of the votes in the Inter-American Development Bank, it tends to vote in a block with the other non-regional members who are largely within the EEC. The combined votes of these delegates can exercise at least some leverage on IDB policies. Thus British delegates to the European Parliament could influence the foreign aid policies of the EEC through the multilateral financial institutions, in the granting of EEC aid (as yet a relatively small amount), and in providing or withdrawing preferential trade treatment to individual Latin American countries.

It is encouraging to see that a Joint European Parliament/US Congress Working Group on Human Rights has now been established, and after a meeting in London in July 1977 has agreed to exchange information, to take part in each other's human rights hearings, and to consult each other on human rights hearings with a view to taking joint action[11]. Whatever the motives and limitations of the current US human rights initiatives, the US Congress has set a precedent for parliamentary challenge and open critical debate of governmental aid policies, and has established a serious institutional framework for carrying out this criticism. At the present moment a parallel framework does not exist either in Britain or in most of Europe, which means that (except in a few isolated cases) parliament and the general public have almost no control over the criteria by which hundreds of millions of pounds of public funds are spent on overseas aid every year.

3. The USA and Guatemala

Brief reference has already been made to the testimony presented in June 1976 to the US Congress, when it held human rights hearings on three Central American countries including Guatemala. The hearings came at a crucial time, only four months after the February earthquake, when Congress had after some

10. *The Times*, 23.6.1977.
11. Joint Resolution of US Congress and European Parliament Joint Working Group on Human Rights, London, May 1977.

hesitation voted an emergency $25,000,000 for Guatemala. At the time of the hearings Congress presented to the State Department a series of questions on Guatemala concerning its assessment of the human rights situation, military aid projections over the coming years, the purpose of military aid and security assistance, and also the sectors at which the aid programmes were primarily aimed. On the question of security assistance, the State Department judged that "the existing human rights situation was not sufficiently serious to raise a question regarding significant reduction or termination of the modest security assistance programmes involved". In the area of economic assistance, the State Department argued that all assistance was in fact concentrated on the rural poor:

In Guatemala, AID concentrates its assistance on the rural poor. However, since the target group is so large, encompassing most of Guatemala's estimated rural populace of four million, it would be impossible for AID to provide all of the support that would be required to ensure significant increases in the general standard of living in a relatively short span of time. For this reason AID attempts to support and encourage Guatemala's own efforts to redistribute resources to the rural poor and to develop innovative and low-cost programmes through which the government can expand basic services. In recent years AID's programme in Guatemala has consisted of an integral approach to rural development with inputs programmed into health, education and agriculture. All of these programmes have been aimed at rural areas and, in particular, the small farmer[12].

As concrete examples the report referred to such projects as the training of health technicians, provision of equipment for clinics and regional hospitals, training institutes and rural primary schools, and the establishment of two cooperative federations providing services to over 65,000 Guatemalan families. It also mentioned programmes which had provided six regional agricultural centres and credit for over 15,000 small farmers.

While there can be no doubt that AID policy has moved more in this direction — the unusually high AID loan of $4,500,000 to the Laugerud-sponsored cooperative movement was a clear indication of the new concentration on small-scale rural development — the motives for the new policies are still open to question. It was seen in previous chapters of this report that the present Guatemalan government is pledged to a policy of carefully controlled rural development, primarily through cooperative growth and the extension of basic services in areas where the problems of unequal land distribution are most acute, and where the dangers of violent insurrection are highest.

During the Congressional hearings, a critical view was taken by two academic witnesses, who claimed that present AID policies are still aimed at peripheral improvements in isolated areas, rather than at programmes which would lead to an improvement in living conditions for the majority of the population. In the words of one of these witnesses:

12. US State Dept., June 1976, responding to questions submitted to the Department by Congressman Donald Fraser (reproduced as Appendix 4 of the US Congressional Hearings, *Human Rights in Nicaragua, Guatemala and El Salvador: Implications for US Policy*).

The military regimes of El Salvador, Guatemala and Nicaragua have not responded to desperate needs for substantial improvements in mass living standards. The moderate economic growth has not ameliorated the living conditions of the lower 50% to 60% of the population. Conditions have in fact worsened in some areas . . . although the need for material improvement cannot be exaggerated, the efficacy of aid is problematic at best. An administrator in El Salvador has pointed out that US aid cannot be expected to produce any substantial, lasting changes in the welfare of the people in countries whose governments are not committed to programmes of improvement of living conditions for the majority of the population. Even aspects of aid programmes which appear directed to improvements of the lot of the majority, are frequently not what they seem. Projects such as Nicaragua's Institute for Peasant Welfare, which had a $14 million US loan, are using as target areas those zones of major guerrilla activities[13].

The same arguments might well be applied to Guatemala where at present a minority of small landowning farmers derives benefit from the cooperative movement, which (as the Guatemalan trade union movement has so frequently pointed out) is usually seen within the country as a conservative alternative to land reform. Likewise, costly infrastructural programmes in health and education have only scratched the surface of the problem, and there are no indications that the level of illiteracy or malnutrition has fallen in recent years.

If criticism of projects aimed at partial improvements seems unduly cynical, it is a cynicism shared by many Guatemalans to the left of the ruling parties. In a country where the US government and its development agencies are seen as responsible first for the overthrow of democracy in 1954, then for the reversal of progressive measures and the destruction of the trade union movement and political opposition, many Guatemalans are unwilling to see anything but ulterior motives in any change of US policies. And up to 1976, when the US State Department had refused to make any public criticism of the Guatemalan government's human rights record but rather sought to exonerate it, it was reasonable to assume that the overall objective of US policy was to maintain internal stability in Guatemala. As in its policy towards other Latin American countries, there are now signs of a change of direction. The US State Department's report on human rights in Guatemala in March 1977 (as one of the 82 countries that had received US military assistance) came at the very time when President Carter was stepping up public criticism of violations of human rights in Latin America. The report, while asserting that the degree of right-wing political violence had decreased during the Laugerud administration, was in other respects highly critical of Guatemala. It observed that arbitrary arrest and torture occurred, particularly in cases involving alleged "subversive activities", and also criticised the failure of the judiciary to act independently in opposing the "extra-legal activities of the executive"[14]. On receiving the report, the Guatemala government immediately

13. From statement by Betty Sumner, Syracuse University, before the US Congressional Hearings on Nicaragua, Guatemala and El Salvador, June 1976.
14. *Human Rights Practices in Countries Receiving US Security Assistance*, report submitted by State Department to Committee on International Relations, House of Representatives, 25 April 1977. US Government Printing Office, 1977.

replied that it would reject in advance any military aid or sale of military equipment from a foreign government trying to impose conditions on matters that
were exclusively the internal affairs of Guatemala. (This response appeared to be
part of an orchestrated Latin American attack on President Carter's foreign
policy when at the same time the governments of El Salvador, Uruguay, Brazil
and Argentina were reported to have rejected any further US military aid as long
as it was tied to human rights guarantees.) The Guatemalan President's public
relations secretary, Roberto Giron Lemus, announced that Guatemala could buy
arms from any country "including the Soviet Union" and claimed that the
Guatemalan police and army had in recent years been using Israeli-manufactured
equipment[15].

This was a further sign that a US government may accept open confrontation
with a 'friendly' Latin American government on human rights grounds and risk
the consequences of its actions. But military aid had reached negligible proportions, compared with the military aid and training programmes of the 1960s and
early 1970s. Projected credits were $200,000 for 1976 and only $15,000 for
1977 under the Military Assistance Programme; and $1,500,000 for 1976 and
$600,000 for 1977 under the Foreign Military Sales Programme[16]. Sceptics argue
that, whatever the attitude of the US President and Congress, extensive government-supported private investment will continue as long as the returns are
favourable. Large industry in Guatemala is almost exclusively US-owned, while
the agricultural export sector is also dependent on the US market. In some
sectors, as in the banana industry, annual profits for US companies are enormous.
One recent report asserts that the Del Monte Corporation (the US multinational
that bought over 55,000 acres of prime agricultural land in Guatemala from
United Brands Company in 1972) made a net profit of $38,000,000 on sales
through its Guatemala subsidiary in 1975; and the Guatemalan Minister for the
Economy is reported to have predicted that Del Monte would recover its entire
investment in Guatemala within three years[17].

In the field of mineral extraction, huge investments have been made by
essentially US multinational companies, backed up by multi-million dollar credits
from official agencies. As of 1974 over 20 major US oil companies had requested
exploration rights in the newly opened up areas in northern and north east
Guatemala, and by 1977 the first large oil wells had been brought into produc-
tion. In eastern Guatemala near Izabal, the large-scale nickel mining project of
EXMIBAL (the Guatemalan subsidiary of the joint US-Canadian multinational
INCO) has sought over $200,000,000 in foreign capital for its initial operations.
Among the finance received by EXMIBAL by the beginning of 1977 was
$15,000,000 from the International Finance Corporation, $13,500,000 from the
US Export-Import Bank, $17,500,000 from Canada's Export Development
Corporation, $6,000,000 from the Central American Bank for Economic

15. Quoted in *INFORPRESS*, 23.3.1977.
16. State Department figures, as given to Congressman Fraser in letter of June 1976 (see
note 12).
17. NACLA Report, *Bitter Fruits*, September 1976.

Integration, $13,500,000 from the US Chase Manhattan Bank, and $13,750,000 from the British National Westminster Bank.

These figures provide a salutary reminder that in Guatemala today bilateral AID funds are an extremely small percentage of total US investment, let alone total foreign investment. At the time of writing an ad hoc group has been set up within the US State Department to coordinate policy on trade and aid questions, and a number of loans to Latin American countries through international financial institutions have already been opposed on human rights grounds. In July 1977 Congress finally legislated that even World Bank loans to repressive countries were to be opposed by the US delegate. But if at some later stage the US government were to oppose loans to Guatemala on human rights grounds, to what extent would this mean the withdrawal of finance from the subsidiaries of US companies operating within Guatemala? In Guatemala, as elsewhere, this may well prove to be the most crucial issue of all.

With the steady rise in private US investment at a time of increasing repression in Guatemala, it is no surprise that the Guatemalan trade union movement in particular has continued to attack the US presence, and continues to see the Pentagon as the arbiter of repressive policies. In the already cited document 'Fascism in Guatemala' (see Chapter III), CNUS attacked US support for a Central American Army, the specialised training that key military operatives were still receiving in the USA and US schools in Panama, and suggested that there were links between the Central American Army and Guatemalan para-military organisations. It claimed for instance that the Guatemalan *Policia Regional* (the secret police whose very existence has been denied by the Guatemalan government) was better known under its name of the Regional Communications Centre (*Centro Regional de Comunicaciones*) which main-tained regular radio links with the US Army Southern Command in Panama. CNUS also attacked the close relationship between the Guatemalan Minister of Labour and the US Labour Attache, and attached sinister motives to the unpub-licised presence of high ranking Pentagon officials in Guatemala in 1977. At the time of the earthquake many people questioned the motives of the huge US military relief operation directed from the US Southern Command in Panama, particularly when this coincided with a massive counter-insurgency campaign in the province of Quiche.

It will take more than a few rebuffs by President Carter and the cutting off of military aid to end the suspicion and hostility to the US presence. Ironically, it may well be the case that the US government's human rights initiative will have least effect in the countries where US influence is currently strongest. To some extent this is because Guatemalan-US commercial relations are largely outside the control of the US administration, but it is also because the US government may be unwilling to cause too much of a breach with those Central American countries that provide the closest and the easiest markets for the United States.

4. The Role of Church and Private Organisations

The human rights lobby within US Congress now demands that the denial of aid should be used as a form of leverage, and that the provision of aid should be used largely to reinforce human rights guarantees (which, to be effective, must entail a degree of structural change). Both these approaches will involve increased contact with church, private and non-governmental organisations. Section 502B of the US Foreign Assistance Act, in requiring that the State Department draw up reports on the human rights situation in countries receiving security assistance, demanded that consideration be given to (i) the relevant findings of appropriate international organisations, including non-governmental organisations, such as the International Committee of the Red Cross and (ii) the extent of cooperation by such governments in permitting an unimpeded investigation by any donor government of alleged violations of internationally recognised human rights. Under Section 116 of the Foreign Assistance Act, the US Agency for International Development has been instructed to consider how human rights factors can influence the structure of the AID programme. Papers on 'Human Rights Factors in Economic Development' have been distributed to AID personnel in relevant overseas countries.

Other aid-donor governments, embarrassed by suggestions that their aid has served only to buttress repressive regimes, have tended to channel more of their overseas aid through private, church and charitable organisations. It is plausibly argued that such organisations take independent policy decisions, sometimes to the point of antagonising the governments of the recipient countries, and are in a better position to see that the aid reaches the neediest. Many European governments (notably the Dutch, Scandinavian, West German and more recently the British) have either allocated a percentage of the total aid budget to private, church and non-governmental organisations; or have provided counterpart funding for projects selected by these organisations.

But in Latin America the small-scale development projects of private organisations have also come under attack if they exist in a political vacuum. The argument is a straightforward and convincing one. Any aid programme designed to produce partial improvements for an isolated group within a repressive society increases its government's credibility and serves only to integrate this minority into an unjust system, often at the expense of the majority. If the problems of underdevelopment are structural, then the inegalitarian structures themselves must be attacked, and the most justifiable role for the outside organisation is to give technical and financial support to those popular organisations which are attemtping to affect structural change.

The logic of the argument can be simply illustrated by looking at the limitations on material and technical aid to small farmers and landless rural workers. Any small farmer will benefit to some extent from increased productivity, but the smaller the farm the less are the possibilities. As long as current disparities in land tenure prevail, then a concentration on productivity alone will bring comparatively greater benefits to the medium and subsistence farmer than to the sub-subsistence farmer and landless worker. But there are cases in which concentration on productivity alone can bring lasting structural changes. In some highland areas of Guatemala it was found that sub-subsistence farmers who increased their productivity no longer undertook seasonal work on the coastal estates, this in turn created a labour shortage which increased the bargaining power of the landless workers. In other areas, where marketing and consumer cooperatives threatened the profits of middlemen and moneylenders, structural changes also followed from the improvement of material conditions.

However, in most Central American countries, including Guatemala, conditions have changed even over the past few years. The landlessness has increased to such an extent that there is rarely a rural labour shortage. Thus an aid policy which improves the conditions of groups of small farmers through cooperatives is to the political advantage of government in that it staves off land reform demands, and reduces the threat to the interests of large commercial farmers.

The most needy sector, the rural proletariat, can be helped only by one of two alternatives, either increased wages or access to land (employment outside the agricultural sector is not a viable alternative in the foreseeable future). In either case it can be argued that their most immediate need is organisation and political awareness (through what has become known in Latin America as "conscientisation"). The concept of conscientisation was originally formulated and popularised by the Brazilian professor, Paolo Freire, a radical philosopher who was convinced that one of the major obstacles to rural change in Latin America was the peasants' lack of critical awareness and consequent inability to understand the true cause of their exploitation. This, he maintained, was partly due to the high level of illiteracy and lack of any opportunity for education and training, but also to the deficiencies of an educational system divorced from the realities of peasant life. By Freire's method peasant groups are encouraged by a specialist educator (who must spend several weeks or months in the peasant community, to acquaint himself with customs and to become accepted by the community) to engage in debate and analyse the reasons for their conditions. The training includes literacy programmes, in which peasants learn to read by concentrating on certain key words relevant to their own environment. After a certain degree of awareness is reached, according to Freire, organisation and practical action will invariably follow, and the oppressed peasantry will themselves seek a solution to their problems[18].

Freire's ideas have had a strong influence on the attitude of sections of the Latin American church, and of many foreign development agencies towards rural development. In many parts of rural Latin America, the Roman Catholic and Protestant churches are the only institutions outside government and political parties which are able to organise development programmes without fear of immediate repression. Training centres have been established, which combine evangelisation with a wide range of courses designed to increase the peasants' awareness of their basic rights, and of the historical reasons for the current violations of human rights. In the absence of legal trade unions these church-based programmes often provide the only opportunity for any form of rural organisation. In most countries this has led to increased identification between sections of the church and the few rural organisations that do exist at a regional

18. Paolo Freire, especially *Pedagogy of the Oppressed*, Penguin Books, 1972.

or national level. In Honduras, for example, the National Union of Peasants (which has now become a serious political force, and has conducted a series of land take-overs after its demands for land reform fell on deaf ears) had its origins in a church-based training programme of this kind.

In Central America at least it is now rare to find any local development agency, church or secular, which does not list conscientisation among its major objectives. Though material benefits are obviously considered important, it is recognised that these improvements must be achieved through an organised group and not in isolation. The underlying philosophy is that poverty is not in itself inevitable, but is the consequence of historical developments and current socio-economic structures. In this sense, human rights and development become inextricably linked.

Church participation in grass-roots organisations has been tolerated by governments as long as militant action has not ensued. Many of the church conscientisation programmes are nebulous and top-heavy, involving very general orientation programmes at the national level, little follow-up at the regional level and limited community action. But in areas where land conflict and social tensions have been most acute and where priests have been directly involved at the community level, the church itself has been subjected to bitter repression. It is no accident that it was in El Salvador, where the priests have been involved in this kind of development work that systematic intimidation and assassination of church personnel commenced recently[19]. And it is no surprise that similar threats against church personnel have been made in neighbouring Guatemala.

When threats of this kind do occur, it can be argued that the external agencies which have funded such programmes have a responsibility to react. Indeed a number of overseas charities and private development agencies, which have abandoned the traditional concept of aid and moved more into the field of human promotion, now accept the necessity for support work for the victims of oppression. This dual role can be seen most clearly in the operation of a large organisation like the World Council of Churches, which combines funding for individual projects (through the Churches Commission for Participation in Development) with outspoken criticism of violations of human rights through its other arms (such as the Programme to Combat Racism). In addition to denunciation, the World Council has concentrated more and more on development projects that have a specific human rights component. A clear example was its extensive support for the church-based Chilean Peace Committee (*Comite de Cooperacion para la Paz*), which combined nutrition and job-creation projects in urban shanty towns with programmes of legal assistance for political prisoners and people who had lost their jobs for political reasons.

In all parts of Latin America, particularly in rural areas, lawyers' organisations can play a similarly important role. The average peasant has neither access to legal protection nor knowledge of the laws of his country or his constitutional

19. *Violence and Fraud in El Salvador: a report on current political events in El Salvador*, Latin America Bureau, London, July 1977.

rights. While legal assistance can sometimes — if rarely — provide a remedy against violations of human rights, legal education can also play an important conscientising role. An interesting view was put forward by the Dutch sociologist Gerrit Huizer in his book 'Peasant Rebellion in Latin America', based on several years fieldwork for the ILO and other international organisations. Huizer maintained that the peasant tended to have an exaggerated respect for the law, and that peasant movements, which always tried first to defend their legitimate interests by appeals to the courts and labour inspectorates, only resorted to direct or violent action when legal remedies failed; but, in the cases of peasant rebellion which he analysed, governments were always unable or unwilling to enforce existing legislation in cases where it protected the peasants rather than the landlord[20].

In Guatemala an organisation offering free legal advice to peasants and poor workers, formed mainly of young law graduates, has received some funding from external sources. It is an important initiative, but it reamins to be seen whether it will escape political repression. When the urban trade unions combined a legalistic approach with militant action, the union lawyers were themselves victims of repression.

Most people tend to draw a distinction between 'development agencies' and non-governmental organisations that exist specifically for the defence of human rights. It can be seen that in the Latin American context this distinction is often a tenuous one. In so far as any useful distinction can be made, it can be said that progressive development agencies play a positive role, giving direct financial support to those indigenous organisations which attempt to fight for their own rights; while the human rights organisations rely more on denouncing abuses to the general public, to governments, and to inter-governmental human rights organisations such as the ILO and United Nations.

If interantional campaigns for the protection of human rights are to become more effective, a bridge must somehow be built between trade unionists, the small groups that work on human promotion in a country like Guatemala and the large international human rights organisations which influence world public opinion. In Central America the development organisations (which have the funds) and the international organisations like Amnesty International and the International Commission of Jurists (which have the prestige) might give their backing to regional lawyers' organisations, and regional human rights bodies in which peasant and trade union organisations are represented. Apart from the degree of protection that this might afford, it might in the long term lead to a broadening of the currently narrow interpretation of internationally recognised human rights.

The very term 'human rights' has inevitably become a subject of political dispute following the Carter initiative. Noticeably both left and right wing in Latin America have attacked the implications of the new Carter policy, sometimes producing the same arguments, but more often arguing on diametrically

20. Gerrit Huizer, *Peasant Rebellion in Latin America*, Penguin Books, 1973.

opposed grounds (the left arguing that the Carter administration was distorting the meaning of 'human rights' by concentraing on civil and political freedoms, while ignoring the violations of economic rights which were a direct consequence of past and present US economic policies in the region; the right arguing that the Carter administration was ignoring the justification for emergency measures, namely the increase of "Marxist subversion" in Latin America). But left and right pursued the same line of argument when claiming that a major contributory factor to violations of economic rights was the unfair prices paid by capitalist nations for the raw materials of Latin America, and the increasing control of the Latin American economy exercised by US-dominated multinational corporations.

The much-publicised report by the US State Department, 'Human Rights Practices in Countries Receiving US Security Assistance', certainly confirmed this imbalance. It was concerned above all with the freedom of the press and the judiciary and with political imprisonment and torture. It was little concerned with trade union rights, and barely at all with the economic rights of the peasantry or with the contribution of US agencies and companies to the establishment and maintenance of repressive regimes (in the circumstances, this was not surprising). In a section on 'Other Human Rights Reporting', the State Department cited only the reports of such agencies as Amnesty International and Freedom House and made almost no reference to the reports of church and private agencies from within the countries where the violations had occurred (whereas an organisation like Amnesty has always claimed that its mandate is severely limited, and that its annual reports cannot be considered an authoritative assessment of all aspects of the human rights situation in any one country). However, until the creation of independent regional human rights organisations which can both assess the situation and attempt to take remedial action, the concept of human rights will continue to be defined by the large international organisations with predominantly 'westernised' attitudes.

5. Conclusions

In conclusion it may be said that there are two levels of the human rights debate: civil and political freedoms at one level, and national and international economic justice at a deeper level. Which ranks first depends mainly on one's political ideology. Meanwhile, it is certain that the urban and rural poor in a country like Guatemala have all of these rights violated at the same time. The decision of the US Administration to accept a narrow definition of human rights will inevitably further politicise the human rights issue, and possibly politicise the work of governmental and non-governmental human rights organisations. It is nevertheless encouraging that the relationship between human rights and foreign policy has been brought into the open, particularly in the US, where it is possible to have public debate on the effects of past and present policies. It is significant in itself that, while the US initiative first concentrated only on civil and political rights, recent Congressional amendments will now compel the US government to take into account the effects of economic aid on social and economic conditions within the affected countries.

But a lot more needs to be done before the US Government's claims even to defend civil and political rights abroad can be taken seriously. In Central America its initiatives have been limited to mild attacks on political repression and the threatened withdrawal of military aid (but in Nicaragua, where recent human rights violations have been fully documented, Congress still approved a multi-million dollar grant in the current fiscal year to the Nicaraguan security services). In Guatemala, where CIA participation in the training of death squads has been widely alleged, the Pentagon and State Department must have more information on the organisation of paramilitary groups than has so far been made available and should itself be able to play an active role in the dismantling of such groups.

Human rights lobbyists everywhere tend to talk more about cutting off aid than about changing its orientation. At the same time the trend in most international agencies is still towards more aid rather than less and this is particularly true after a natural disaster like the Guatemalan earthquake. One of the first things to become apparent after it happened was that external agencies found it impossible to allocate funds efficiently in many affected areas because there were no organised groups through which reconstruction programmes could be established. One large British charitable agency had been funding a rural development programme in the area most affected by the earthquake and was able to use the personnel employed in this programme to establish an efficient and large-scale distribution, first of food and medicines, later of urgently needed reconstruction materials. In other more isolated areas, where there were no foreign-funded development programmes, the local inhabitants (unable to participate themselves) had to watch the representatives of foreign development agencies draw up their own reconstruction programmes without regard for local opinion. At the governmental level, the initial stages of the earthquake relief programme were controlled by troops from the US Army Southern Command.

The Guatemalan earthquake again reflected the vital need for organisation at the grass-roots level before construction or reconstruction programmes could be efficiently carried out. In some international forums, and in most private aid organisations, this need is now recognised. Thus, while the trade unions and the organised labour movement in Guatemala continue to be attacked as politically "subversive", the ILO adopted its recent Convention concerning the role of rural workers in social and economic development. It is however a sad comment on official aid programmes that, despite the professed concerns of the inter-governmental labour organisation, only a few private organisations have been willing to give active support to the labour movement and speak out against systematic trade union repression in Guatemala. Over the past few years the British trade union movement has shown outstanding solidarity with the workers of Chile. But Chile is only one of many similar countries. This trade union concern must now spread to other areas including South and Central America.

Abbreviations

AI	Amnesty International
AID	US Agency for International Development
BANDESA	National Agricultural Development Bank
CGTG	General Confederation of Guatemalan Workers
CIDA	Inter-American Committee for Agricultural Development
CNT	National Confederation of Workers
CNUS	National Council for Trade Union Unity
CTF	Confederation of Federated Workers
EGP	Guerrilla Army of the Poor
FAO	UN Food and Agricultural Organisation
FAR	Rebel Armed Forces
FASGUA	Autonomous Trade Union Federation of Guatemala
FUR	United Revolutionary Front
IDB	Inter-American Development Bank
ILO	International Labour Organisation
INCAP	Nutrition Institute of Central America and Panama
INTA	Institute of Agrarian Transformation
MANO	National Organised Anti-Communist Movement
MLN	National Liberation Movement
ODM	UK Ministry of Overseas Development
ORIT	Inter-American Regional Organisation of Workers
PGT	Guatemalan Workers' Party (Communist Party)
PR	Revolutionary Party
UFC	United Fruit Company

Conversion Table

Area

1 caballeria = 111.5 acres
1 manzana   = 1.7 acres
1 cuerda   = 0.1 acres
1 hectare   = 2.47 acres

Weight

1 quintal   = 101.4 lbs